D0120577

Also by The F2

F2: World of Football

F2 FOOTBALL ACADEMY

Published by Blink Publishing
3.08, The Plaza,
535 Kings Road,
Chelsea Harbour,
London, SW10 0SZ

www.blinkpublishing.co.uk

facebook.com/blinkpublishing
twitter.com/blinkpublishing

Paperback – 9781788700207
Ebook – 9781911600077

A CIP catalogue of this book is available from the British Library.

Cover design by Nathan Balsom
Internal design by Leard.co.uk
Printed and bound in Italy

1 3 5 7 9 10 8 6 4 2

Blink Publishing is an imprint of the Bonnier Publishing Group
www.bonnierpublishing.co.uk

To The F2 Family, old and new.

THE F2 APP

GET THE ULTIMATE FOOTBALL SKILLS GUIDE FREE ON YOUR SCREEN!

Billy: Download our free F2 App and you'll be able to see our skills come to life on your device.

Jez: That's right, we've packed in new, never-before-seen video tutorials and helpful tips, so you can learn how to play like a pro. And once you've honed your touch, you can upload your own skill videos and share them with us!

Billy: To access all this exclusive content, download the free app from the iTunes App Store or Google Play Store, launch the app and point your device's camera at the pages with the special phone icon (right). Then sit back and watch the magic happen!

Jez: It's that simple, so what are you waiting for? Download, read, watch, learn and take your game to the next level. See you on the football pitch!

*The F2 App by The F2 requires an Internet connection to be downloaded and can be used on iPhone, iPad or Android devices. For direct links to download the app and further information, visit www.blinkpublishing.co.uk

Scan this page now for your first video!

CONTENTS

Welcome to The F2 Academy. We're the professors, this school is in session, and here it's permanently game time. In this book, we will help you take your football skills to the next level. We'll also take you further into our world, sharing with you what goes on behind the scenes at The F2.

In our 'Get the Skills' sections, we'll teach you some incredible skills and unreal tekkers. Want to be the best on the field when you're playing with your mates? Study our lessons, train hard and you'll soon be playing like a pro.

For the full F2 experience, don't forget to download our incredible free app with exclusive 'how to' videos and extra tips to supersize your skills. But it's not just about upping your game, it's also about upping your swag – we'll show you how you can dress and talk like a star.

It's been an eventful year since our first book came out, *F2: World of Football: How to Play Like a Pro*. So, we'll give you the lowdown on what we've been up to. We've made videos with superstars such as Luis Suárez, Mauricio Pochettino, Lionel Messi and Lewis Hamilton, travelled in Brazil, the USA and Europe, and met lots of you guys all around the world.

There have also been challenges, including injuries and the passing of a figurehead of The F2 family. We're going to reveal to you the full story on everything that has happened – it's been intense.

We'll also chat about some of our favourite Tekkers Masters, discuss ways to improve your understanding of the game and a whole lot more. This is a true freestyle feast.

So, here's the opening whistle, signifying the start of the book. Turn through the pages, be entertained, learn loads and feel inspired. We love The F2 family and we want you to all be the best you can be.

Love, peace and tekkers,

Billy and Jez, aka The F2

F2
CHAPTER
ONE

PLANET F2: FREE KICKS WITH RONALD KOEMAN!

We teamed up with the Everton boss Ronald Koeman to film a variety of free kicks. He was a master of free kicks back in the day, slotting them home for Ajax, Barcelona and the Dutch national team. What a legend. He gave us tips and advice. The film was for a kick smoking campaign, which we were proud to be part of.

Jez: We've filmed with so many players and some managers over the years, but it's different when you meet a manager to when you meet a player, isn't it?

Billy: Yeah, well, gaffers are used to giving players the hairdryer treatment, aren't they? They have that authority and power. They're serious people and management is a serious business, really. Whereas the players are a bit more liberated – the managers give them days off to enjoy themselves. Of course, even for players football is still a serious game, but ultimately they're doing their hobby as a job and they're absolutely loving it.

For managers, it's different. Just look at the media – the pressure on gaffers is unreal and it can feel like everyone is trying to ridicule them and pull them down. So, it's a totally different life for them.

I don't really get nervous when we are going to meet players, whoever they are. But with managers I can get a tad twitchy. Footballers generally really like a laugh, but a lot of managers don't – they're really seriously focused on the quest to win the next game. That's all they care about.

Koeman, though, was brilliant with us.

Jez: That's right. The thing about managers is that the ones at lower levels, say Sunday league managers or school coaches, they tend to have an ego: they're the gaffer, they're in charge. They're the boss. They can be a bit power happy about it.

So, at the lower level they really try

to assert their power more – they're always reminding you that they're the gaffer. Whereas, what I've found with managers at the top level is that they're so much the boss, they do not need to explicitly assert their power. Everybody knows that they command that respect. They are the boss – it's not even up for a moment's debate. They don't feel the need to prove it. They can walk gently but carry a big stick, as they say. I actually think that if you have to say you're the boss then you've lost control. Top-level bosses are often just nice, really nice. I didn't know exactly how Koeman was going to be with us, but he was really decent. It was a good shoot.

Billy: The idea of the video was for him to give us tips and advice on how to take free kicks. Not from a technical point of view, but tips such as where you should aim in the goal, which side free kick-takers go, and for what reason. That was the shape of the video, really.

I mean, look, we're not beginners, we take free kicks already. But what he did do was give us an insight on another technique: not where to aim in the goal, but where to aim over the wall. It's a lot easier to aim for a section just over the wall than it is to aim for a section in the goal – because the goal's obviously 25 or 30 yards away, but the wall is only 10 yards away. So, he gave us a position between the second and third man, to whip it over towards the near post. He said: 'If you always aim between these two guys' heads, above them, then your line is right.'

We tried it to see if it works and it does. It makes free kicks so much easier to score from. It was incredible: if the goalkeeper lines up his wall correctly, the second man should always be in front of the near post – if you get it over his head, your line is always going to be right. This was a really interesting insight for me.

Then he started talking about the reverse: keepers always think you'll go over the wall to that near post, so he said occasionally you can whip it over to the far post. As he said it, I tried one. It was an absolute peach. The keeper had stepped to the right and he got flat footed. The ball hit the side netting first. I was well happy with that one.

Jez: There's a lot of science in it all.

Billy: A lot of trickery, too. He developed this great technique where he went really side on to the ball and managed to get the ball up and over the wall. The thinking behind this is that keepers knew that he was going to target that near post most of the time, but they couldn't react before he went because every now and then he would reverse it and go to the other side.

The keeper would think: 'He nearly always puts it at the near post', but then he'd dink one to the other corner and the keeper would look silly. So, the keeper can't commit until he's hit it, but by then it's too late for the keeper to get across to the other side.

Jez: If you haven't played at the top level it is easy to underestimate the mind games that go into it. Not just in football, in other sports, too. It's like in boxing, one guy might do a little feint, just to see what the opponent does when he does that. In most sports, there's a really big psychological element that goes on. It's like a game of chess.

So, for example in football, when a player steps up to take a free kick or a penalty, most people won't notice those subtle gestures, those little nuances, which the taker sends out to the goalkeeper. Most fans and viewers won't pick up on that, but it's all going on. Players who have played at the highest level know that it goes on and they can see it. To the participants this is a proper thing. It can make the difference. It was interesting hearing from him about the mind games that go on before he takes a free kick.

Billy: He told us so many fascinating things. He said that after training he would stay behind and practise free kicks for two hours. David Beckham used to do the same thing, and you can see the results.

You could see the results in Koeman's career, too. He was the top-scoring defender in world football. He was also Barcelona's top-scoring defender, with 90 goals in all competitions. He was absolutely deadly from free kicks and penalties.

This takes us back to the whole Ronaldo v Messi debate. If you look at Ronaldo, he worked so hard to get where he is. Whereas with Messi, it's kind of more natural, he doesn't seem to have to work so hard to get there. It's like he's already there, which is amazing.

But full credit to those players who do work so hard. It shows real determination and sets such a good example. Koeman himself is a good role model, I think. He was really down to earth – a nice guy.

Jez: That's right. As for the message, smoking is just one of those habits that is simply not healthy. We loved being able to get a positive, helpful message out there without looking down on people who smoke for whatever reason. It wasn't about being judgemental, it was about saying that if you do want to quit, this is the most effective way to do it: by seeking help from a healthcare professional. It was good to be part of a campaign that really helps people.

Billy: There's nothing better than giving out a positive message in a video. You can't be involved with smoking as a sportsman. We all know how damaging it is and how it risks your very life. I think it's good that so many kids now are so smart and switched on. It was an honour and a pleasure to do that video. Jez and I have never smoked, there's no benefit from it – just damage.

F2 ACADEMY: SCIENCE OF SWAZ

HOW TO TAKE THE PERFECT PENALTY

Jez: We actually filmed a penalty video with Mark Noble. We asked his secret for taking spot kicks. He told us to focus on hitting the target first, rather than worry about goalkeeper. Decide that if you're going to fail, you'll fail by a save, not a miss.

Because if you miss the target, that's your fail. But if you get it on target, even if you struck it poorly, you might still score, because the keeper might make the wrong move and let it through. So, your first priority must be to hit the target. Flash or not, doesn't matter. Just hit the target.

And you know what? Mind games kick in here. Big time. Your first mind battle is against yourself. That starts when you're practising. Make it so you are mentally comfortable going both sides. Train your brain to feel relaxed about it, because that way, you have more options on match day.

If you've only practised shooting a

penalty one way, then you're always going to kick it that way, even if you know the keeper is going that way. So, master going both ways. Then, when it comes down to it, you've got the luck on your side more.

Next, comes stage two of the mind games. Practise with a good goalkeeper. Try and learn if there are any 'tells' – little signs that give away which way they're going to go. You could try a bit of eye deception: look at one side, hinting you're going to go that way but then slot it the other way.

Obviously, out and out lying is not a good thing to do in life. But the truth is that in sport, if you can deceive your opposition, that is a positive thing.

It gives you the edge. So, there are areas where you should learn to be the master of deception. And penalties are one of them. Go for it!

F2 ACADEMY:

HOW TO FINESSE YOUR FREE KICKS

KNUCKLEBALL

Jez: I love the knuckleball. How I love the knuckleball. So, what is it? It's striking the ball with minimal spin or top-spin. Strike it with back-spin or side-spin? That's not a knuckleball. Get it with no spin or top-spin? That is a knuckleball.

You punch the ball without follow through on your foot. It's like hitting it with a knuckle – that's why it got its name. The object of this trick is no spin. The reason is that if the ball isn't spinning as it goes through the air, it moves very unpredictably. Turbulence and air pressure causes the ball's journey to deviate randomly.

Just as the pilot can't predict what will happen with turbulence, the kicker of a knuckleball can't predict what will happen. Neither can the goalkeeper. Even if he's been catching balls his whole life, he can't catch it because he can't predict the path of it. That's why it's so popular, but it's very, very difficult to master. What's important is what part of the ball you strike – and what part of your foot strikes the ball. Watch how Ronaldo runs up to the ball on his tiptoes; that can help because your foot needs to be pointing downwards. Hit the ball with your inside bone.

Gareth Bale and Cristiano Ronaldo are among the players who have nailed the knuckleball. Watch them do it and you'll see that you don't need much power on the strike, but you do need a whole lot of accuracy.

There is maximum swag with the knuckleball!

Billy: When you get a free kick anywhere near the goal, you've got a lot of options as the taker. Whippage is a very good one – just ask Lionel Messi.

Messi loves a bit of whippage, just watch him bend that ball home. He approaches the ball from a slightly different angle – more side on. He hits the ball with his instep – that's crucial. You also need to make sure you land on the foot that struck the ball, not the other one.

The whippage is more reliable and consistent than the knuckleball, but don't dismiss the knuckleball. When it comes off, it's cool. It's up to you to choose which you prefer.

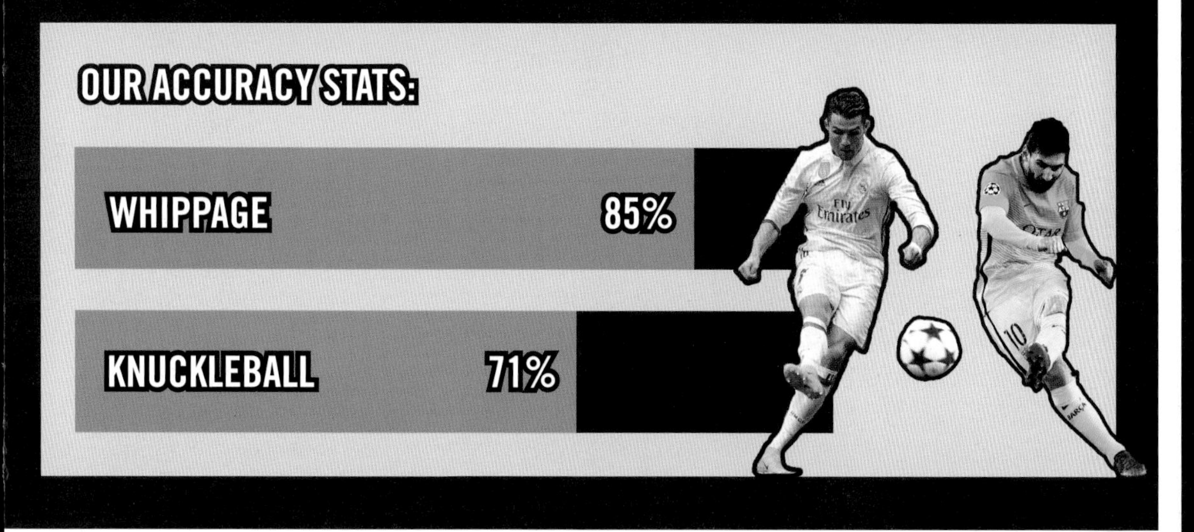

F2 ACADEMY:

Jez: Top-spin is a great way to outfox your opponents – it looks awesome too.

For this one, you should strike the ball in the bottom half. Aim for slightly to the opposite half of your kicking side. So, if you're right-footed, hit it slightly left of centre.

Hit the ball with the inside of your foot for top-spin. Hold the foot as rigid as possible during the follow through.

Use this one to send a bit of excitement through the crowd and your team-mates.

PING

Billy: We love a bit of ping! And we're in good company. Guys like Pirlo, Gerrard and Beckham have been the masters of ping over the years. The ping combines distance, precision and accuracy.

This one is all about the technique – not the power. Approach the ball at a 45-degree angle. It should be sweet – the ball should fly like an arrow with zero curvage, but a dash of back-spin.

GENERAL FREE-KICK TIPS

1. Focus at one point above the wall
2. Focus on the second and the third person in the wall
3. A left footer should aim between the first and second person in the wall
4. Stand side on to the ball as you prepare to take it
5. Four to five steps in your run up can work well – but go with what feels comfortable
6. Lean to the side when you kick the ball
7. Get your toe up over the ball if you want to go for whippage
8. You can't practise too much

TEKKERS MASTERS:

ALEXIS SÁNCHEZ

'HE NEVER STOPS WORKING, AND HIS ABILITY IS SECOND-TO-NONE. BUT HE'S ALSO A LEADER.'

Jez: This guy is on a different level to most players. I think that's linked to his upbringing. He comes from very humble beginnings, so his work ethic is unbelievable. He's got a bit of everything, hasn't he? He's got an unbelievable shot, he can do knuckleballs and that's what we'd do with him – knuckleballs. We love Alexis Sánchez.

Billy: We really do. As we write this, Laurent Koscielny is captain of Arsenal and he's doing a good job, to be fair. But I would 100 per cent give the captaincy to Alexis Sánchez if he stays there. I'm putting that on the line. I'll tell you why: I remember when I watched him in the 2-2 draw between Arsenal and Spurs. I love Alexis, I love him for everything he does on the pitch.

Jez: Even as a Spurs fan?

Billy: Even as a Spurs fan. Doesn't matter who you support – quality is quality. He never stops working and his ability is second-to-none. He's also a leader. Sometimes people don't notice his leadership abilities, but if you watch, and I focused on just him for 10 minutes of the Spurs match, you can see what he does.

I like to watch players when they are off the ball, because that's when you can gauge how good they are. So, I kept my eyes on him and his movement was incredible. But the main thing was that he was talking.

He was communicating non-stop to his team-mates, telling them to do this, to do that. To go here, to go there.

It was brilliant to see! When he was giving these instructions it was with an anger, like: 'This what we have to do NOW!' It was as though I was watching a manager on the pitch, which says to me that his football knowledge is immense.

Jez: Wow.

Billy: So that's why I'd go so far as to say he should be Arsenal's captain. He should wear the armband for Chile, too, and for whichever club he's at. They should build the team around him in every sense. He is a leader, so why not make it official? Just because he's a skilful player and quite small, that doesn't mean he can't lead. He can.

Jez: I think him and Mesut Özil are the best Arsenal players, but there are lots of differences between them. Özil makes the players around him look

'SERIOUSLY, HE'S SO GOOD. I'D GIVE HIM THE ARMBAND IN A HEART BEAT.'

better than they are, whereas Alexis makes the players around him look a bit worse. He doesn't intend to, but I think he does do that. It's his class.

I saw him once at an event but I didn't go up to him. I was leaving just as he was arriving. Lots of the top players know who we are now, but even so, I didn't want to bother him as he might not have ever heard of us.

He's always been high on our list to make a video with and we've heard that he's interested in making a video with us and his dogs.

Billy: Seriously, he's so good. I'd give him the armband in a heartbeat.

Jez: Yeah, we remember you saying.

Billy: Shut it, you. I think with him as skipper you'd quickly see how he can bring new things to a team. Everyone likes Alexis Sánchez, don't they? I don't know anyone who likes football who doesn't like Alexis Sánchez.

GET THE SKILLS:

RONALDO ELASTICO

FACT FILE

ORIGIN: INVENTED BY CRISTIANO RONALDO
SKILL TYPE: DRIBBLE
DIFFICULTY RATING: 8
TEKKERS RATING: 9
FREQUENTLY USED BY:
CRISTIANO RONALDO, RONALDINHO

Jez: Imagine being a defender and facing up against the great Cristiano Ronaldo: you have to deal with the pace, power, and, of course, the masterful trickery of one of the greatest forwards the world has ever seen – it must strike fear into the hearts of even the most seasoned stopper. You never know what he's going to do next: a feint here, a shuffle there – anything to leave you with twisted blood.

In fact, it seems as if he invents a new trick with every game! Check this one out – the Ronaldo Elastico. Need to beat the last man on your way to goal? Simple: just pull this one out of the bag and leave them in your wake. This one is all about quick feet – so make sure you practise it as many times as possible before trying it out in a match.

APPROACH THE BALL ON YOUR TOES
TAP THE BALL WITH YOUR STRONGER FOOT...
RUN ON TO THE BALL

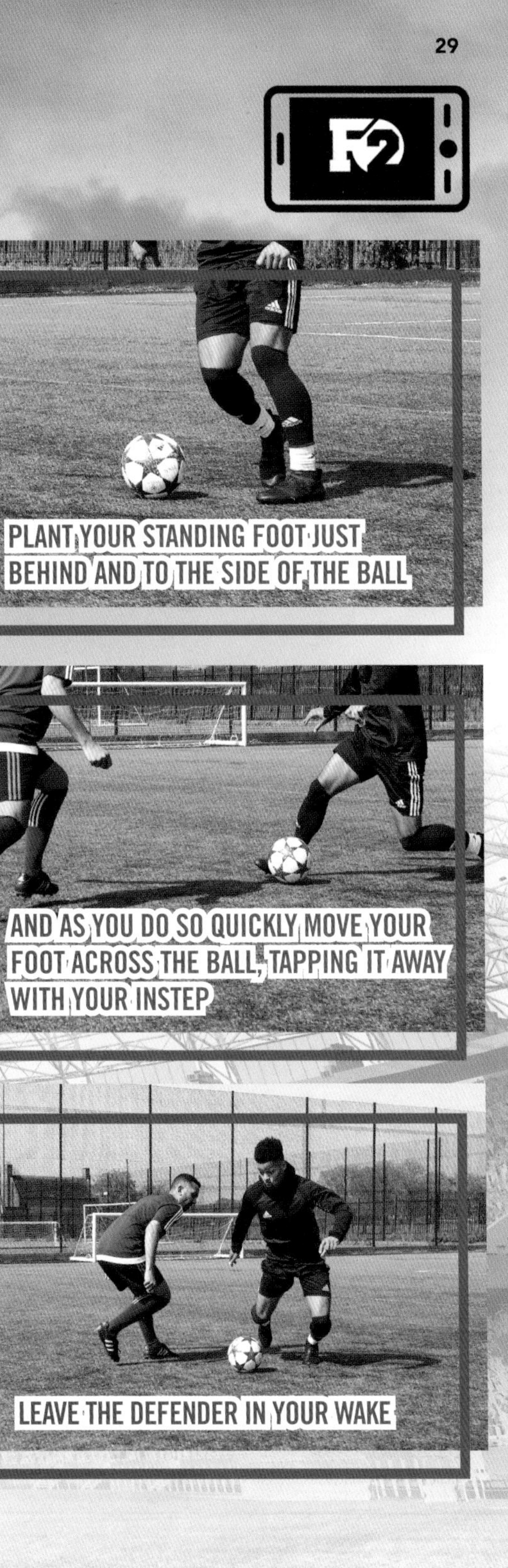
PLANT YOUR STANDING FOOT JUST BEHIND AND TO THE SIDE OF THE BALL
AND AS YOU DO SO QUICKLY MOVE YOUR FOOT ACROSS THE BALL, TAPPING IT AWAY WITH YOUR INSTEP
LEAVE THE DEFENDER IN YOUR WAKE

adidas
KEEP ON YOUR TOES
PUSH THE BALL WITH YOUR STRONGER FOOT
BRING YOUR FOOT ACROSS THE BALL

KNOCK THE BALL WITH YOUR INSTEP

adidas
adidas

CHAPTER
TWO

PLANET F2: THE MONACO GRAND PRIX!

Check this: we got to watch the Grand Prix in luxury and hang out with one of the planet's most famous sportsmen. It was unreal.

Jez: You know, when we first heard about this gig I could hardly believe my ears. The whole thing sounded like a dream. I mean, from the start, you know when you're going somewhere like Monaco that it's going to be sheer class.

Before we knew it, we were on the flight. Let me tell you, when we arrived we were treated like kings. Absolute luxury from start to finish! To get the ball rolling, we were escorted to the Formula One Monaco Grand Prix in a helicopter. How cool is that?

We were taken to a prime spot, overlooking the track. It was all laid out for us there. There was champagne on ice. There were fashion models. And the Grand Prix was going on down below. Nice.

This was the first time I heard F1 cars in person, the first chance in my life to discover how they sound live. I'd heard so much about what an experience it would be. I'd had it on my bucket list for so long. I had always thought: 'I don't know how but I want to experience Formula One in person before I die.'

It was great. To be honest, I probably thought it was going to be a bit louder than it actually was, but overall it was everything I hoped it would be. We had the full experience of the cars whizzing home right beneath us. It was absolutely incredible.

Billy: It was. We were staying in luxury pad with champagne, with canapés being handed around – the works. After the race, we got our cars back to the hotel. This wasn't just any hotel, it was a £20k-per-night hotel. A spa in the hotel, a sea view – all the Monaco trimmings! All the things they gave us, it was amazing.

We had a shower and got changed, then we went to a reception at the best restaurant in the area. We had

champagne with gold inside it – actual real sprinkles of gold. Who drinks champagne with sprinkles of gold in it? How is that even a thing? We didn't drink too much of the golden bubbly but we did try a glass. Apparently, the gold comes out the other end! Which is a shame, given how much gold is worth.

Jez: I've got to be honest, I didn't like it that much.

Billy: I noticed you still had a glass, though.

Jez: Well, it would be rude not to!

Billy: Then there was a smart meal, before we were whisked off to Lewis Hamilton's table at a nightclub. Now that was a surreal experience. All the F1 drivers were at different tables and there we were at Hamilton's table. Unfortunately, he didn't show up because he was already at a prior engagement – with Justin Bieber of all people!

But who cares? We were at the top table in the club, surrounded by the elite of Formula One. And we had a proper adventure ahead of us the following morning.

Jez: Exactly. All that was just day one.

Billy: The next day, we jet-skied to Lewis Hamilton's yacht. It was about a 20-minute jet-ski across the coast to the yacht. Lewis was there and he just chilled with us for the whole day. There were drinks and food all laid on. Banging music playing as if it was a nightclub.

Jez: That jet-ski journey was harsh. It was choppy water that day so it was far from ideal conditions. When you come down off a wave you properly crash down. If you'd just had your breakfast, it's going to re-emerge, believe me. I got salt in my eyes; my eyes were proper weeping. Not comfortable at all, but it was a definitely an experience.

It was well worth it. At the end of it, we're on a yacht with the guy who won the Monaco Grand Prix – Mr Lewis Hamilton! He was such a relaxed, chilled guy. Absolute quality. I hadn't been quite sure how he would be because I think he's misrepresented a lot in the media.

He likes a fun lifestyle off the track. Just because he's like that off the track, it doesn't mean he's anything less than focused and professional on it. I think that's great, but some people will misjudge it. However, for me, if someone decides to work hard and play hard, I've nothing but good to say about them.

He was really welcoming, chatting about football, chatting about Formula One. We asked him about nerves and how he plays it behind the wheel. He's really good on jet-skis so him and Bill had a bit of banter about that.

It all felt so natural – it was just like being with a mate. I hadn't expected him to be so real, because he's such a superstar. Yet he came across as a normal guy, just one with a very, very extraordinary talent. We were with him for three to four hours.

Billy: Lewis Hamilton is so down to earth, he really is. He's a calm character, as it goes.

We also did some fly-boarding, when you're propelled above the water. A jet of water goes up and you

have to balance on it, 12 feet above the water. It sounds extreme and it is. Jez was useless. I wasn't so bad. It was funny watching Jez, though.

Jez: Harsh, Bill, harsh. Okay, let's try and break this down a bit more fairly and accurately, shall we? The fly-boarding was amazing. But I've got a little problem – I can't dive. I just never learned as a kid. With those fly-boarding things, what goes up must come down. And the higher you go up, the bigger the drop. You come crashing down.

Now, if you can dive that comedown is a reasonably graceful thing, with no pain involved. But with me, whenever I was coming down, it was different. I'd panic and brace myself for impact. I came off feeling like I'd been beaten up. So, my advice to anyone thinking of doing this is twofold. Number one: do it, because it's fun. Number two: learn to dive first.

Billy: Fair play, Jez. I won't rip you too much about it. Then we said goodbye to Lewis, jet-skied back to the shore, got a car to the airport and flew home. I couldn't have dreamt of such an experience as a little kid. It's so surreal the position our careers have put us in.

When you're a kid you never think you'll end up in that position, because how would you even get there? How we've managed to make a career that brings brands and famous people into our world is unreal. You never expect to be on a yacht with Lewis Hamilton.

Jez: We'll remember every moment of that trip for as long as we live.

F2 ACADEMY:

HOW TO DRESS LIKE A PRO

Jez: My first rule is this: no boot-cut jeans. Ever. Just don't!

I think, actually, everyone has got their own different style. I also reckon it's easier for kids to be stylish these days because of Instagram. You can follow stylish people and fashion pages, and you can pick up tips from them.

But also make sure that you be yourself. Take tips, ideas and inspiration from others, but be yourself too. Don't try to be anyone else. And remember: no boot-cuts!

Billy: Part of football is getting slaughtered by your team-mates over your clobber. That's the same from school, through to Sunday League and the professional game itself.

Express yourself, experiment with styles – and expect a bit of banter!

TEKKERS MASTERS:

GERARD PIQUÉ

'KIDS CAN TAKE SO MUCH INSPIRATION FROM HIS JOURNEY, THEY REALLY CAN.'

GERARD PIQUÉ

SPEED: 9
VISION: 8
TOUCH: 8
FINISHING: 7
TEKKERS: 7

F2 TRUMPS

Jez: Right from the off, I want to say something big about this guy. Kids can take so much inspiration from his journey, they really can. Sir Alex Ferguson saw Piqué as not quite ready for Manchester United, so Sir Alex let him go – but then he went to Barcelona and became the kingpin of their defence. Now, who is more respected in the game than Sir Alex Ferguson? Probably no one. There's certainly not many others who are up there with him in stature. He's like a guru. Yet he was willing to sell Piqué on. Did Piqué let that destroy him? No, he fought on and went to Barcelona.

Now, he's won more than any Manchester United player and become one of the biggest talents in the world! He's won a World Cup, a European Championship with Spain and countless trophies with Barcelona. He is one of just four players to have won the Champions League two years in a row with different teams. Talk about decorated: he must need a whole room in his house just to keep all his medals and caps in.

Billy: The trophy room! What a story, mate, what a story.

Jez: So, what can we learn from all of this? The best managers in the world can make mistakes just like the best players can. If Sir Alex Ferguson can get it wrong with a player then a school coach or Sunday league gaffer can too. So listen, readers, if you get

told you're not good enough, don't let it destroy you. Don't be discouraged. Keep your head up, keep your confidence high. Remember Piqué – and keep trying.

Billy: He's one of the most technically gifted centre backs in the world – if not the most. He suits Barcelona down to the ground because all he wants to do is play football – and that's the Barcelona way, isn't it? He's bang on their message and right in their brand!

You know what? I don't think I've ever seen him punt the ball up field. He's not a hoofer. He always wants to play it out from the back. He feels confident enough to play on the floor, he must be one of the most assured players on the pitch. To have that confidence to play with such grace in such a dangerous part of the pitch is quite something.

Jez: Yeah man, his confidence levels must be through the roof and that reflects in everything he does on the pitch throughout the 90 minutes. As a player, he's not the quickest, but he doesn't need to be because he's very intelligent. He uses his brain and that means he can outfox players who are faster than him physically.

Billy: He's just such a nice, friendly guy who simply loves playing football. All players love the game to an extent, but there are sometimes one or two players here and there who take that love to new levels. It's a pure love.

What you have to understand is that everyone in the game loves football, but for players it is their job. They are literally professional footballers. Pressures come in to play, there's a lot at stake – like your livelihood, the fans and so on. That can change things for some players: they go from just loving the game to feeling they have to succeed for professional or financial reasons. The water can get muddied.

Players like Piqué are different. They don't see the game first and foremost

'I SEE HIM AS THE ULTIMATE MODERN DEFENDER.'

as a job; they see it as a passion. Their mentality is that they want to win and also enjoy it. They stay focused on the essence of the game.

Jez: I see him as the ultimate modern defender. He's got strength, passing ability and just top-notch technique. He's good in the air and can also offer the team plenty going forward. He's like two players in one, in that way. Maybe even two and a half.

Billy: Or three?

Jez: Steady on, pal!

GET THE SKILLS: SÁNCHEZ HOCUS POCUS

FACT FILE

ORIGIN: INVENTED BY ALEXIS SÁNCHEZ
SKILL TYPE: DRIBBLE
DIFFICULTY RATING: 8
TEKKERS RATING: 9
FREQUENTLY USED BY: RONALDINHO, NEYMAR, ALEXIS SÁNCHEZ

Billy: Defenders always worry when Alexis Sánchez has the ball – they never know what he's going to do next! In fact, I don't think there are many other players in Europe right now with so much x-factor – not even he knows what's coming next. You can tell by the way that Sánchez plays that this trick is purely instinctive. There's a real element of surprise to it that even the best defender won't be able to predict what you're going to do. The Hocus Pocus sums Sánchez up perfectly: quick, instinctive and pure, unadulterated Tekkers.

The key is quick mind and quick feet: make the decision to perform the trick and stick to it; then let your feet do the rest. Try and keep your eyes on the defender too – it'll help with your positioning and your timing.

F2

KEEPING ON YOUR TOES, PLANT YOUR WEAKER FOOT IN FRONT OF THE BALL
AND ACROSS YOUR BODY

WITH THE INSTEP OF YOUR STRONGER FOOT, ROLL THE BALL BEHIND YOUR STANDING FOOT...

...AND PUSH IT IN FRONT OF YOU

HOOK YOUR FOOT AROUND THE BALL...

SPRINT AWAY FROM THE DEFENDER

PLANT WEAKER FOOT IN FRONT

FLICK BALL BEHIND AND PUSH THROUGH

F2
CHAPTER
THREE

We travelled to Brazil to film a pilot for a new subscription platform called YouTube Red. We wanted to capture what football meant to the nation of Brazil. We visited the beaches, the favelas, the mountains and worked with locals, some of the world's best freestylers and futsal players and some of the up-and-coming Brazilian stars who teach themselves through the art of street football. To say the trip was eventful would be an understatement…

Jez: Brazil is a beautiful place. We loved the weather and the scenery. The horizons are like nothing I've seen before. The clouds come down over the tips of the mountains. There's something about that – it looks incredible to see them intertwined. There's quite a lot of that in Brazil. I loved it.

The glamour and the rhythm of the place are magical. You have to go there to even begin to appreciate how great it is. Listen, if you get the opportunity – take it!

Billy: It's the home of football and maybe the home of tekkers too. Football is so meaningful to the people in Brazil. I'm not even sure there are the words to do justice to how important it is to them over there.

How can I put it? Football is more than a sport out there, it's a passion. Actually, maybe, it's more than a passion, it's a religion. It's just so, so good to see, wherever you go, football is played everywhere by everyone. They play with such joy and freedom. It's so incredible to watch. It's something else, it really is.

Brazil has got the most successful national team in the history of the World Cup. They've won five titles, and come in second place, third place and fourth place twice each. No one has touched that.

The guys who make it through to play professionally, often have had to battle poverty, drugs and crime. Life can be hard in some areas of Rio. Football is their only escape, their only way out of a bad situation. But they seemed happy. They are with their

family and friends, so I'm not saying they hate their life. They don't. They are happy people, but they know that football can open up the world and let them escape to something better.

What an incredible experience it was to visit Rio – it's a beautiful city. I'd been once before when I went to a soccer exhibition. But I didn't get to see the place that time. That time, I literally flew in, went to the event and then flew out the next day.

So to spend time there making that film was great. The visit was not without drama though…

Jez: You can say that again.

Billy: Our aim was to go there and be in a position where we could film in all the places: the good, the safe, the bad and the dangerous. We wanted to witness how the people live and what they experience and their culture. So, we went to the favelas – these are like shanty towns. All the homes are packed together supertight – it's like a maze of streets and alleys.

We took security with us, we were paying them £10,000 a day to look after us because some of the favelas just weren't safe.

For example, there was a guy with a gun on a rooftop who was really intimidating us because he felt we were on his patch. There was also a gang who told us we had to stop filming and get out of there. Jez and I had to make a swift exit. The security guy's face was a picture – he was literally terrified. When you see that sort of expression on the face of your security, you know it's time to split.

Here's how that went: the pitch was right next to this shack and that is where the gang hang out. They're all about 18, 19 or 20. As soon as we started filming this guy stood up on the roof and started watching us. It was so intimidating.

The guys in Brazil said that this was their way of saying: 'You're on our patch, you're not in control.' The security guard suddenly ran up and said: 'You've got to stop filming now!' So, we ran out of the area. We were only 20 minutes into filming. It was scary.

The security guard said: 'Listen, I've been doing this job for 20 years, and my job is to keep you safe.' He was saying:

'I'm telling you – don't go back down there.' But the fixer was telling us: 'I know these guys, they're just trying to intimidate you – they won't hurt you.'

Jez: It was really awkward.

Billy: There we were in the minibus and we had two different sides of advice. The fixer was saying 'Go for it', the security were saying 'Don't'.

In the end, I just concluded: 'Look, I've got kids. I'm not putting myself in a situation where I risk my life for a bit of extra footage.'

Jez agreed right away. So, we both pulled out. We had to change the whole filming. It was still an incredible experience, though, to go down there and film that.

I'll never forget that moment when they came running out and said: 'Put the cameras down, put the cameras down'. We had two security men, one of them was a military police officer who is known in that area. He couldn't even come with us because if he got recognised he could get shot. That's how wild it is in the favelas.

The other one said: 'You can't tell anyone down there that I am a security guard. If anyone asks, just say I'm a sound guy.' He didn't want to be a target either. So, he had to negotiate with the locals as if he was a sound guy. It was all just so hostile.

Jez: I remember feeling like our very lives were in jeopardy. Like anything could happen. We could be shot or kidnapped. I just felt powerless. Even the police don't step into those areas. It was all very uncomfortable.

As Bill said, we had a security team but only one of them felt able to come down there with us. I wasn't that happy with that, for a start. The one that did come down – it didn't take long at all for him to announce that we had to go. He said, listen, things have taken a turn for the worse. You have to leave. But some of the production crew wanted to get some extra shots.

I thought, we all want this to be good, but there is somewhere you have to draw a line. And I think this is an important point for kids: always go with your gut instinct. You have a gut instinct for a reason. It's a real thing and it's wise. I don't know the science behind it, but every time I've had a strong gut instinct it has turned out to be right. The only times I've gone against it, I've ended up regretting it. Sometimes you just know it's about to kick off, even though there is no objective evidence for it. I felt that times one hundred. We were out of there. We were targets, weren't we? A prime opportunity for troublemakers. Social media is our world, anyone big on there could be a prime target for baddies.

Billy: Then we had someone throw broken tiles at us from four storeys up. Imagine the crashing sound that it makes when someone throws tiles from that high up. It's terrifying. It smashed into a hundred pieces. If just one of them had hit Jez it could have done him amazing damage or even killed him.

Jez: That was awful. Wow. Porcelain tiles thrown from 50 feet up in the air. Aiming at me. One came really close to me, it just missed my head and smashed on the ground. I could tell from the angle it bounced at and the power of the bounce that it hadn't just casually fallen off – someone had thrown that.

So, I said to Billy: 'I think someone's thrown something at me.' Literally seconds after that, another one came down. Bang! I was out of there. I wasn't going to get my head cut open or worse.

After a while I went back and it happened again. This time no one was in any doubt what was happening. We all rushed off. And, get this – the camera crew weren't even filming at that point so it won't even be in the episode. What a downer. I mean, if you're going to nearly die, at least get the footage. Ha, ha!

Billy: The favelas are beautiful places, though. Obviously, they're dangerous. But there's something so brilliantly simple about life in them. That simplicity has a beauty to it, I feel. All the people are really connected with their neighbour. In modern-day society that isn't always the case. But over there, there's a togetherness about it that is so special. So, let's be fair.

Jez: I'd agree with that, I'd agree with that. There's a lot of poverty out there. But there's plenty in London and LA, too. The spirit in Rio is unbelievable. But that favela where they threw tiles at me? I'll never go back there as long as I live. Would you?

Jez: Listen, we mess up, man, we mess up. We've got to hold our hands up, we do that. We've actually made a point of showing that we mess up. We put videos out with our fails because everyone messes up, we're all human. We want to be honest with our audience. We don't want anyone thinking they're less of a person or a player if they make mistakes. We all do.

Billy: That's why we started putting out the 'fail' videos. It's important that kids know that they will make mistakes but it's how they respond that counts.

Jez: Half the time we find it funny if we make a big mistake because it's not the norm. It's hilarious if it's a big fail. It's like when you speak and your voice comes out all squeaky. It's the same when you make a big mistake with a football. Just learn to laugh with it and learn from it.

That's it. The path to success is littered with mistakes. If you're not making mistakes, you're not trying hard enough. So, don't beat yourself up if you get something wrong – just sit down and analyse what you could have done better. And next time – do that thing!

PAUL POGBA

James Milner sent the corner in and Pogba conceded a penalty with his handball. People compared his handball to his dab.

ROBERT PIRES... AND THIERRY HENRY

When Arsenal got a penalty against Manchester City, Pires and Henry tried to recreate a penalty made famous by the Dutch tekkers legend of old, Johan Cruyff.

In an appearance for Ajax, Cruyff passed his spot kick to his on-running team-mate Jesper Olsen, who teased the keeper out before passing back to Cruyff who tucked it in. But it all went wrong for the French Gunners when they tried it. Pires didn't kick the ball properly, meaning he couldn't touch the ball again according to the rules of the game. There were red faces all round!

F2 ACADEMY:

MARIO BALOTELLI

We're big fans of Mario and there is no doubting his talent. He's pulled off some tasty tricks on the pitch but watching him try – and fail – to put his bib over his head time and again was hilarious!

NANI

Check this one out: Luís Nani had to apologise to Cristiano Ronaldo – his own team-mate – after denying Ronaldo an epic goal in Portugal's defeat of Spain in 2010.

Ronaldo was on fire. It looked as if he had put Portugal ahead when he turned inside Gerard Piqué and then sailed his shot over Iker Casillas. So, imagine how annoyed he was when Nani sped in from an offside position to head the ball in from point-blank range. The goal was disallowed!

And did you see what happened? Ronaldo was so annoyed he threw his captain's armband on to the pitch! Woah!

RONALDO

But Cristiano himself has made some mistakes. In his Old Trafford days, he once did so many step-overs that he tripped over. He outfoxed himself!

TEKKERS MASTERS: SERGIO AGÜERO

'HE'S JUST THE ULTIMATE STRIKER, ISN'T HE? HE'S SO STRONG, QUICK AND LETHAL.'

Jez: This guy is such a great example to kids who are learning the game. You can tell he's spent a lot of time practising his shot. He's not just a powerful shooter – he's deadly accurate. Consistently.

Billy: Yeah, you can only get to that level by practising with super-human dedication.

Jez: Everyone sees the skill now, but it's the hours and hours you put in to it that count. It's not just the work you do on the big stage in front of the world, it's the shift you put in when no one is watching, when there is no glory. You just work and work to improve yourself, so you're ready when the millions are watching.

He is a player who should be of particular inspiration to small kids. Because Agüero might be small, but he's strong. He's strong, strong, strong. He's not even human in a way, he's more like a machine – you can't push him off the ball. So, if you're reading this and you're a bit small, keep going. If Sergio Agüero can do it, then so can you.

Billy: He's just the ultimate striker, isn't he? He's so strong, quick and lethal. You give him half a yard and he gets a goal. That makes it so hard to play against him. For defenders to try and shut off that half a yard for 90 minutes is impossible. He's one of those guys who will win you titles. Who could forget that goal in the last minute of the 2012 season that beat QPR and won the Premier League for

Manchester City for the first time ever? Manchester United were practically ready to celebrate when the news came through: City snatched the title from their biggest rivals! No wonder he's so highly valued on the world stage. If or when he decides to leave City, he's going to command such attention and such massive numbers.

He's played as a second striker sometimes and he's definitely versatile, but I like to see him as an out-and-out striker, I think that's where he is most threatening. Tactically, he's sharp as a knife, his vision and passing are amazing, but it's in front of goal where he does the damage. He's also quick, shrewd in his positioning and just has top-drawer technique.

Jez: I reckon he's so agile, too. He's also got amazing acceleration, as many opponents have discovered to their cost. He stays on the balls of his feet when he speeds off. He's just an absolute menace – the complete striker. He's got it all: touch, awareness and vision. He pulls the trigger the moment the opportunity arises. He's bold. Agüero and Suárez are probably the best two strikers in the world right now. Diego Costa on his day is up there as well, but in terms of consistency, those two stand out.

Billy: Another amazing asset he has is that he doesn't look like a destroyer, does he? He's lethal, but he doesn't look it. You could call him a silent assassin. He's little and cheeky-looking. He looks harmless, but he can destroy you. He gets goals, he's really intelligent with his movement and has an unbelievable shot too. He'll make runs that confuse defenders.

Jez: He's lethal. And yeah, even though he looks like a really nice, friendly guy, on the pitch he is deadly. Like I said, you can see how hard he's worked on himself: he has really close control and breathtaking dribbling skills. He's also got more natural, organic qualities: quick feet and the strength to keep the ball.

Billy: You can compare him to some of the best players of the last 40 years: Diego Maradona, Romário, Alessandro Del Piero. He's got a bit of what all those guys had – I'd actually put him in their company to an extent.

Jez: You can't pay a player a much higher compliment than that. He's one of those players it's good to listen to. When he talks about the game he talks a lot about two things: finding space in the box and paying attention to what's going on. The two go together. He's there, sharp as anything, watching what's going on and ready to react the moment he sees an opening. A true predator.

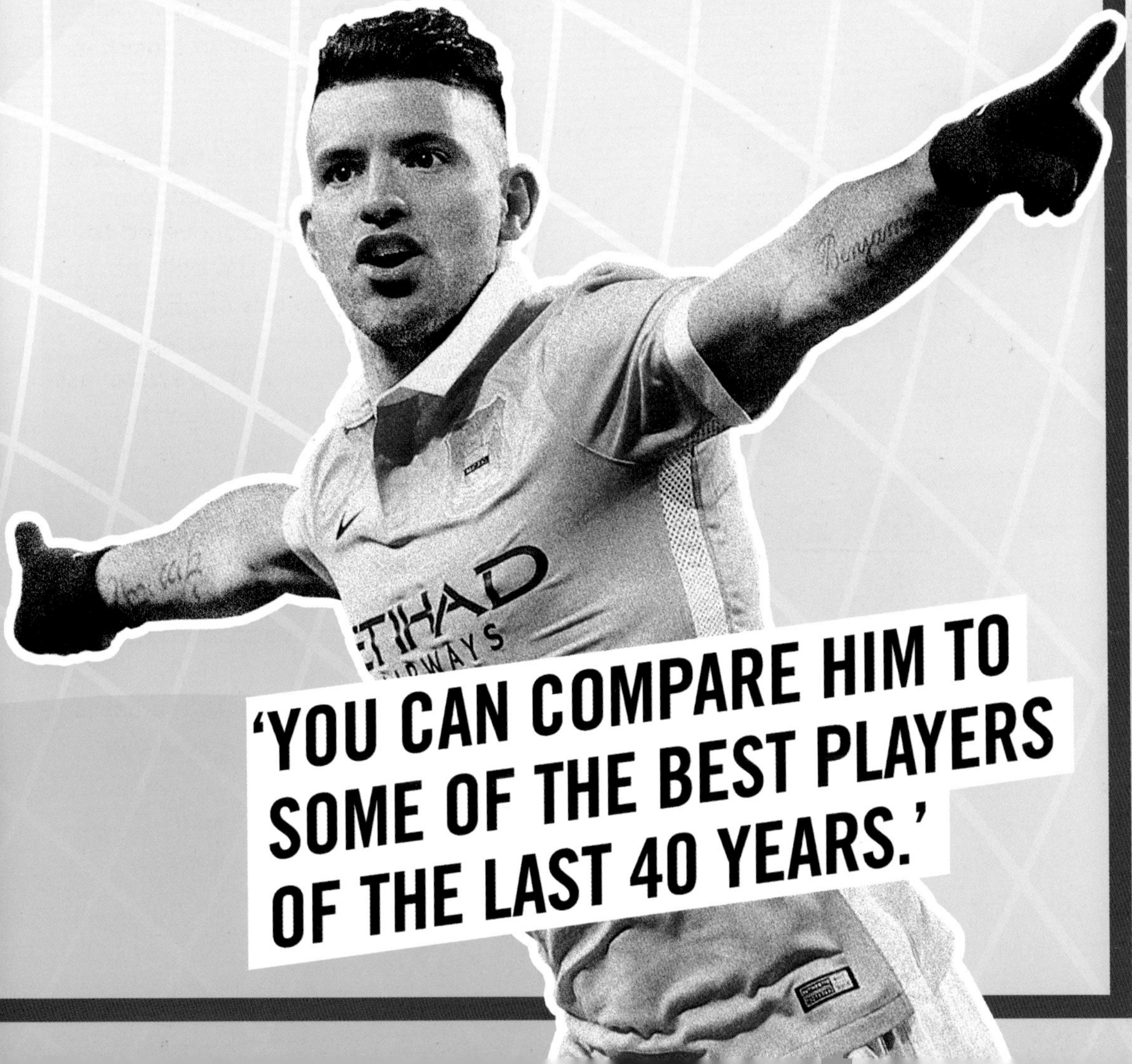

'YOU CAN COMPARE HIM TO SOME OF THE BEST PLAYERS OF THE LAST 40 YEARS.'

GET THE SKILLS:

NEYMAR RAINBOW FLICK

FACT FILE

ORIGIN: UNKNOWN
SKILL TYPE: DRIBBLE
DIFFICULTY RATING: 6
TEKKERS RATING: 8
FREQUENTLY USED BY: NEYMAR, RONALDINHO, ALEX IWOBI, DOUGLAS COSTA

Billy: There are tons of names for this one: the reverse flick over; the Lamretta; some of the older ballers even call it an 'Ardiles Flick'. For me and Jez, though, there's only one proper name for this piece of Tekkers, and that's the 'Neymar Rainbow Flick'.

Our favourite Brazilian is fond of this piece of skill, which is perfect when getting out of tight spots – I remember Neymar used it in a game when he had a couple of defenders around and it called for drastic action. Keep in mind, though, that you need to make sure you get a good trajectory with the ball – so that means height and enough lift to get it beyond the defender. Then it's just a case of 'see you later...'

PRACTISE PLANTING YOUR ANKLES FIRMLY AROUND THE BALL

POWERFULLY FLICK YOUR LEGS BEHIND YOU, PULLING YOUR FEET APART ONCE YOU BEGIN TO DESCEND

CONTROL THE BALL AND SPRINT AWAY

JUMP WITH THE BALL BETWEEN YOUR FEET

THE BALL SHOULD SCOOP OVER THE DEFENDER AT A GOOD HEIGHT

APPROACH THE DEFENDER WITH THE BALL

PLACE FEET FIRMLY EITHER SIDE OF BALL

POWERFULLY SCOOP BALL INTO THE AIR

CONTROL AND SPRINT AWAY

Championship
MANAGER17

CHAPTER FOUR

Billy had an operation on a hernia and Jez had an operation on his ankle. Both operations put us out of action for over four weeks. A terrible time…

Billy: My problem with the hernia was a nightmare and there are still problems around my hip. I need to really warm up now. The operation made a big difference, but it was a tough time in the weeks afterwards. Looking back, I feel like I went through a bit of depression.

Check it from our perspective: our job is to provide awesome content for millions of people. Then suddenly I found I couldn't do it. For about six months I was filming and playing with an injury. That's really hard, it becomes difficult to enjoy it. You don't want to talk about it because you don't want word getting round. So, you just try and battle through it but every single filming day becomes just that – a battle.

I'm left-footed so every time I hit the ball I was in pain. I had that for six months and then Jez had an ankle problem for a year and a half. If his ankle went he'd be rolling around the floor in total agony. Then my problem started to get worse quicker.

Everything seemed to be accelerating down a path that we really wanted to get off. So, we both decided to bite the bullet and have our respective operations at the same time. They told each of us we'd be out for four to six weeks.

Jez: For me, a piece of bone was there for about a year and a half. At the front of my ankle. It was just floating around in there. Every time I pointed my toes, it was just moving around. It was excruciatingly painful.

Amazingly, The F2 had been going for about four years when I got that operation. So, do the math: for nearly 50 per cent of the time The F2 had existed, I had been working at 60 per cent of my potential. Staggering sums.

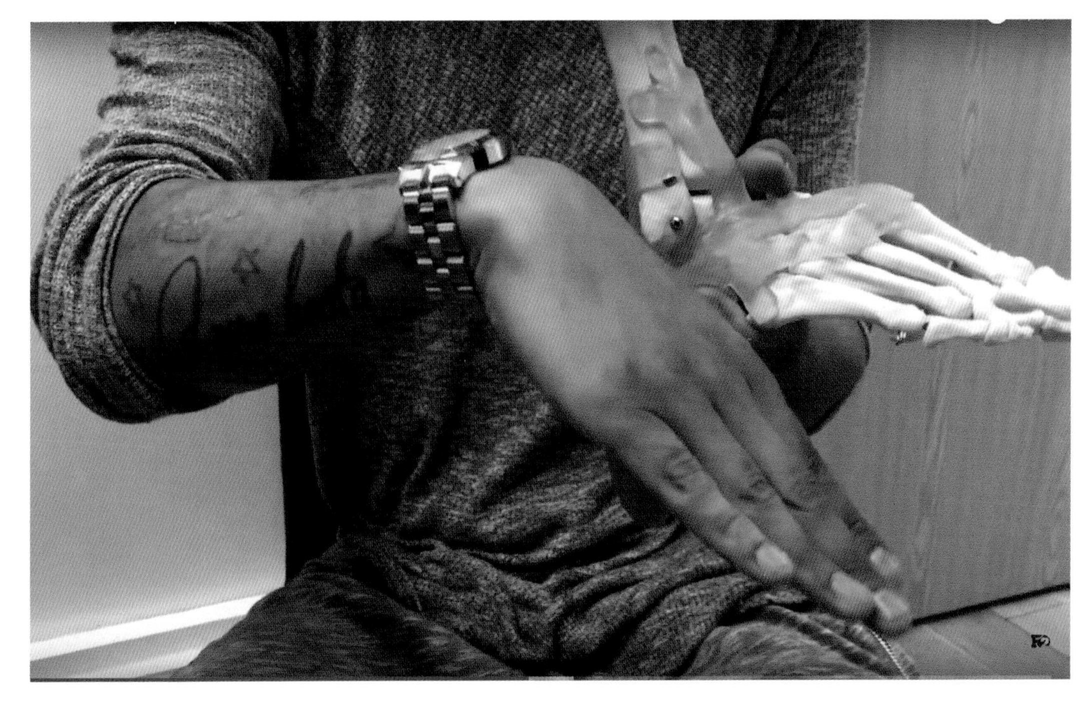

All this meant that if Bill crossed the ball to me I could no longer volley the ball. I'd end up on the ground in terrible, terrible pain.

There were lots of different techniques I couldn't do. I couldn't follow through. It was really, really limiting. In the cold it was even worse. Man, I hated some of those days in the cold. There were times when I'd go down in agony and we'd have to stop filming.

But the surgeons said that surgery would put me out for four to five weeks. If I'm out for that length of time, it means The F2 is out for the same time. This would mean Bill wouldn't be able to work or earn money during that time. It would have cost us a lot to take the time out.

More importantly, it would have cost us five years of growth. You can lose your momentum on YouTube in an instant if you lose focus. It was the worst time. We're the biggest independent football YouTube channel. But back then we weren't at the top.

So, I kept pushing through it with my ankle. Gritting my teeth and doing the work. But then Bill got a hernia, so he had to have an operation. Making it the perfect time for me to get my operation, too. It was ideal, to minimise loss.

Billy: We'd built up until we had a really good following, strong growth and so on. And then that kind of stops. As Jez said, you worry that you will lose momentum. Part of the success of having YouTube and building a fan base is consistency of uploads. People who don't upload consistently don't build such a base.

We were worried whether our fans would stay with us. It was a really, really hard time. It really was.

Jez: People said to us: what, you both got injured at the same time? That

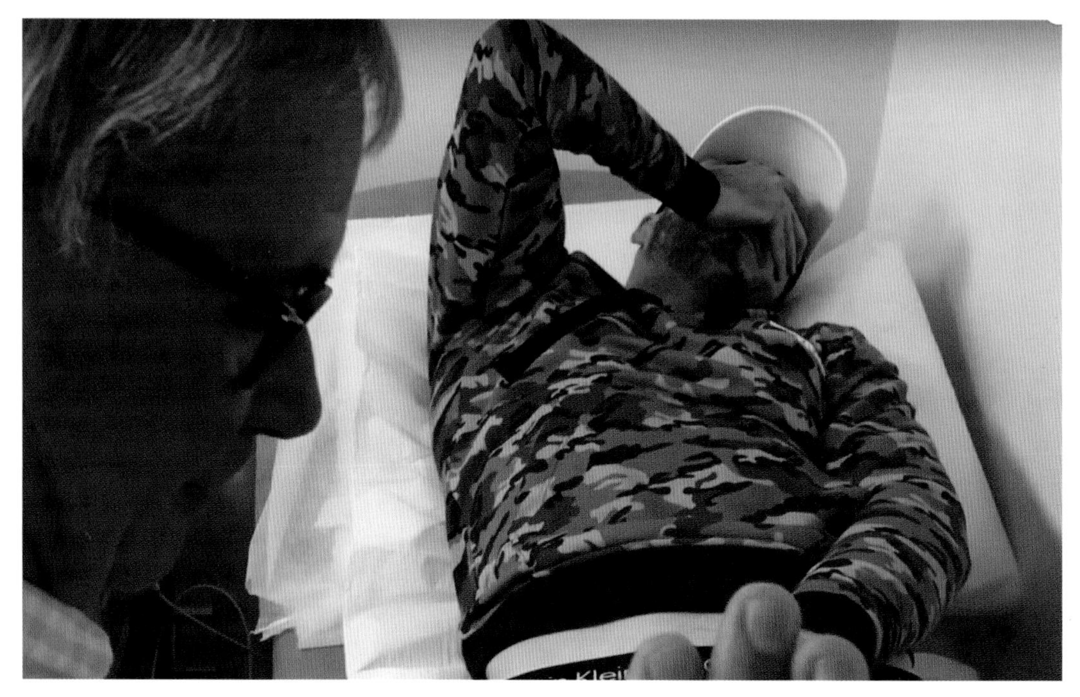

doesn't sound legit. But we didn't get injured at the same time at all. I'd been injured for 18 months before Bill got his hernia. I just didn't want to knock out our momentum for five weeks.

So, we had our operations and we got through it. We made some vlogs about the injuries and the operations. I thought we should let the fans see what was going on. That was important. These were basic videos, just using my phone, but they came out really well. They were insightful. It was nice to have that different type of video. So people can feel they are with us.

I was a bit scared when I had to go under general anaesthetic, I must admit. I'd never been under it before. I don't like needles anyway, but there's a funny story for you here. I'd always wanted to see how long I could stay awake after the anaesthetic was in me. I was curious, and my competitive side kicked in. I was determined to film it and see how long I could stay awake after it was administered.

I asked if I could film and they said no. But, after he injected me, I started counting. I was proper shouting: 'One… two… three… I'm still awake… four… five… still here…' I was even making my eyes go wide open, just to add in that extra way of buying myself more time to not go under. They were so wide – I must have looked like Mesut Özil as I lay there shouting away!

When I woke up after the operation, the first thing I asked was: 'How long did I last?' The doctor started laughing and he said: 'Well, how long do you think you lasted?' I said: 'Hmmm, I'd be happy with nine!' Because everyone had said I'd not last beyond six. He said: 'It was 17, you lasted until 17!' He said: 'You were shouting, "I'm still here! I refuse to go to sleep!"'

He said it was the funniest thing he'd ever seen in his life!

There's been so many great strikes to enjoy this past year. There are plenty of babies we've had to leave out of this list. Which have you enjoyed?

EDEN HAZARD V ARSENAL

Billy: I loved it when the Belgian mastermind dribbled from his own half and then finished against Arsenal in February.

Jez: Mate, even as a Gooner I had to take my hat off for this. The key to this solo striker was his fine ball retention.

Billy: He showed real nerve, too. If you watch again you'll see Coquelin was trying his hardest to stop him, but Eden didn't let that put him off his stride. Then he dummied and shimmied past Koscielny and slotted it home.

Jez: What a player.

ANDY CARROLL V CRYSTAL PALACE

Billy: Everyone likes a bicycle kick and this was one that was so class it could win the Tour de France.

Jez: That's so true. Look at the faces on the defenders and goalkeeper after he netted it. Ha-ha, get on your bike, son!

Billy: It's a nice cross and he has found himself some space on the edge of the defensive pack. His balance to pull it off is first class.

HARRY KANE v EVERTON

Billy: How good is this guy? He gets a lot of praise but I can't help wondering if he'd get a little more if he played for Manchester United or Barcelona.

Jez: If he carries on scoring goals like this, it won't be long before those sorts of clubs come knocking. The absolute venom in that strike was borderline filthy! Lashing it home from 20 yards he beat Joel Robles at his near post.

Billy: Notice how, before he shot, he found himself plenty of space. He ran with the ball for a while, waiting for the right time to shoot. Class.

OLIVIER GIROUD v CRYSTAL PALACE

Jez: Look, big Oli G's finish here was exceptional. A perfectly executed scorpion kick. But let's rewind a bit because he was key in the build-up, too. He did a neat lay-off on the halfway line and then absolutely belted towards the area.

Billy: Yeah, that was a proper lung-bursting run. And even after he'd done that, he was still poised enough to see his chance with the scorpion and to pull it off with such panache.

Jez: Credit to my man, Alexis Sánchez, for the cross. But the main praise has to go to Giroud. Look, his beard may be a bit too thick, but when he can score goals like that, who cares?

F2 ACADEMY:

HENRIKH MKHITARYAN v SUNDERLAND

Jez: This goal came on Boxing Day and it was a present to anyone watching it.

Billy: Well, maybe apart from Sunderland fans. But, yeah, it was quality.

Jez: Big Zlatan sent a cross into the box, and then it was just absolute madness. Mkhi dives forward and hooks the ball behind him into the far corner.

Billy: Which scorpion was better: his one or Giroud's?

Jez: So hard to call it, but I'm going with Oli's. He had to work harder to make it happen, plus his was onside. Ha, ha, big up Giroud!

Billy: Predictable from a Gooner, but I'll let you have that one.

PEDRO v TOTTENHAM HOTSPUR

Billy: This curler was a beauty but we should take a moment to discuss the context. Spurs had gone 1-0 up in the eleventh minute and with just seconds to go before half-time, they could be confident.

Jez: Then this happened. Pedro has thrived under Conte and no more so than here. He curled it into the top corner with aplomb.

Billy: A game-changing goal. Spurs were stunned and Chelsea went on to win.

Jez: A nice celebration, too. I've got a lot of time for players who stick their tongue out to toast a beautiful strike.

Billy: Swag!

DIMITRI PAYET v MIDDLESBROUGH

Jez: You can't do a list of great goals and not include a solo effort. I love it when a player gets the ball and just goes for it, doing the whole thing by himself.

Billy: This was a perfect example of the solo goal: Payet got possession on the left, spun past Barragan and then cleverly weaved his way across the goal, biding his time as he danced past four defenders, before coolly angling in a shot.

Jez: It's been a testing season for the West Ham fans in various ways, but in that moment they must have been buzzing.

Billy: What a talent Payet is – they'll miss him.

GASTON RAMIREZ v AFC BOURNEMOUTH

Jez: This is the solo goal to end all solo goals.

Billy: Yes, mate. It's not often that a side gets a goal as a result of a corner they conceded, but that's what happened here. After Boro faced the corner, Ramirez blocked a shot and then picked up the loose ball in his own half.

Jez: Then he's done that stunning run into the Bournemouth penalty area, cut inside the defender and side-footed the ball home.

Billy: An almost Messi-like moment!

Jez: Yeah, I'd agree with that, I'd agree with that.

TEKKERS MASTERS: DELE ALLI

‘THIS GUY HAS SO MUCH PASSION, HE NEVER WANTS TO LOSE.’

Billy: Here's another talent we spotted early. We filmed with him when he very first signed for Spurs. When we're filming with a player, we reckon we can gauge how good they really are. We believe we can gauge what level they're on and going to be on. When we filmed with him we'd never seen him play, so we went into it not knowing what sort of player he was. But on the day, we saw his ability. He was up for anything. I came away from it and I said to Jez: 'He's amazing, he's got the full package.' Jez said: 'Yeah, he's got everything.' Even from a one-hour kickabout, we could see that he's got all the technical attributes to be a top player. And I mean a top player.

It was just a question of whether he could transfer those skills to match day – and it turned out he could. So, we're saying that we called it early: Dele Alli is a stunning player. We can't exactly say we scouted him, but we can say that we spotted it.

Jez: Yeah, we could see right then that this guy was going to go far. You could just tell. He seemed so complete. He was so comfortable with whatever we asked him to do. As an all-rounder, he was outstanding on the day. He's quite a tall kid and it doesn't do him any harm.

Billy: We had lunch with Pochettino once and we chatted about Alli. Listen, he rates Dele beyond what you'd believe. He said: 'This guy has so much passion, he never wants to lose. You don't get players with that mentality any more.' It's like the Steven Gerrard

mentality – that aggressive need to win that burns in them.

Can you imagine what he'll be like in three years? He'll be bossing the Premier League. Or La Liga, if that's where he is!

Jez: Yeah, he's going to do well in the game. Remember that in his first full campaign at White Hart Lane, he was voted the PFA Young Player of the Year. And look at what the guys who have won that honour have gone on to do. It's been won by Glenn Hoddle, Ian Rush, Gazza, Ryan Giggs, Robbie Fowler, Beckham and Rooney.

Billy: And Cristiano Ronaldo and Gareth Bale. Eden Hazard, too.

Jez: So that's a signifier for you right there, that's the shoulders he's rubbing with. He can score and create, and do so much more, too. Central midfielders (CMs) seemed to get more goals in the past. Nowadays a CM who can score seems to be a rarity. Players as tall as him are rarely so well balanced, either. He's fast and stronger than you would think to look at him.

Billy: Watch how he can drop back, collect the ball from defenders or even the goalkeeper and then get an attack going. He's tireless and so clever. He's also got a good spring on him and

'CAN YOU IMAGINE WHAT HE'LL BE LIKE IN THREE YEARS? HE'LL BE BOSSING THE PREMIER LEAGUE.'

that, combined with his height, makes him a threat in the air.

Jez: I also think he makes good decisions. He picks the right pass or the right shot. He's one of those players who reassures fans – when he picks up the ball you feel he isn't going to waste it.

With his anticipation, he will always be a step ahead of those around him. That means he draws fouls from opponents. When that's near the box, it can be a real gift for team-mates who love to have a go from a set piece.

I can actually see this guy doing really well for England in the future. He could become a proper pivot for the national side.

Billy: No wonder Pochettino rates him so highly – and no wonder that we, The F2, spotted his talent so early. Hold your applause, we don't want praise. What can we say? I guess we've just got a special eye.

Jez: As an Arsenal fan I'd rather players like Alli and Kane played for us. We've had things all our own way for so long in our half of North London but now our rivals are looking tasty. But with my neutral head on, I'm glad to see young English guys like those two coming up in the game.

GET THE SKILLS:

PAUL POGBA HALF VOLLEY

FACT FILE

ORIGIN:
SKILL TYPE: SHOT
DIFFICULTY RATING: 6
TEKKERS RATING: 8
FREQUENTLY USED BY: PAUL POGBA

Billy: The half-volley is all about timing: too early and the ball will sail over the crossbar; too late and you're lucky to make any connection at all! The trick is to plant your standing foot just before the ball bounces up and strike its sweet spot at its optimum height.

Watch Paul Pogba: his half-volleys are all about timing, placement and power. Improvisation is key – you need to take into account where you are on the pitch, how hard the ball bounces and where the keeper's standing. Master that and then add the swaz. Get out on the pitch and get practising!

KEEP YOUR EYE ON THE BALL AT ALL TIMES

AS IT FALLS, TURN SIDEWAYS ON

PLANT YOUR STANDING FOOT AS THE BALL BOUNCES, SWINGING BACK YOUR SHOOTING FOOT

FOLLOW THROUGH WITH YOUR BOOT

1
1
1
adidas
AND WATCH THE BALL...

ASCAL
adidas

CHAPTER FIVE

No words can express what a loss it was when Bill's father passed away. We want to talk about what an amazing man he was.

Billy: Straight after our injury nightmare, something happened that put it all in perspective – my dad died. It was such a devastating experience that it made being injured seem like nothing in comparison; it made injury seem a treat in comparison.

I thought I'd had it bad with an injury, but then when Dad died I thought: 'What I wouldn't give to have him back. I'd take any injury in the world for just one more day with my Dad.' When someone passes away it makes you realise what is really important in life.

The pain continues for me, I have to admit. It's had an impact on The F2 work, too. Jez and me like having a laugh and banter when we are filming. That's part of what The F2 does, isn't it?

But in the months since my Dad passed away, I was really struggling to get into the zone for that aspect of our videos. I actually didn't feel like I wanted to be joking around. I still love filming tekkers, but the humour part has been harder for me since we lost my dad. I feel like there's something missing in me. I'm not having as much banter as I used to. I'm trying, but I'm not sure when I'll get it back.

Losing a parent changes everything. You can wake up some days and think: 'I don't want to film today, I don't want to do anything.' You can't stop thinking about what's happened. I'm sure my whole family would say the same.

It's been the worst situation in my life. I know people say time is the biggest healer but it's slow. As I write this, I've got to the stage now where I will have good days and bad days, whereas for the first months afterwards it was only bad days and bad days. There were no good days back then. Every day I woke up and felt terrible.

That was just the way it was.

I don't even know how I came through it. It was a rollercoaster. It's not like you're suddenly better. With bereavement there are ups and downs and it's all so unexpected. So, my next challenge is to have more good days.

How I do that is by remembering as best as I can that my Dad loved what I did with football and The F2. He was so proud. So, I'm trying to use that as strength. I'm using that as a positive. My Mum has said to me several times: 'He'd want you to get out there and carry on. He'd want you to show The F2 family what you can do.'

I can honour him by doing that.

Jez: You can. Tell them about your tattoo, my man.

Billy: I've had a tattoo done in honour of my dad. I've never wanted a tattoo in my life but then I got one for Dad. It's Roman numerals of the day he passed away. It's on my arm.

When I first got it done, Jez said: 'Do you want to get that on your arm? It seems so negative – to have the date of the worst day of your life. Do you really want that on your skin?'

So, I said: 'Jez, the way I'm looking at it is a bit different.' The thing is, the message behind the date is to remember that any moment something so precious can be taken away from you. I want a reminder of that, so I don't ever take life for granted again.

If I can use this date to wake up in the morning, look at my arm and think: 'I'm going to be the best I can today' then that will be a positive. I'm trying to turn that awful, awful day and make it a motivation to thrive and to grow. A permanent reminder: don't take anything for granted because you can lose something in an instant. Things can change in a second. So, just be the best you can be in everything you do.

Jez: I get you.

Billy: I've got to say, Jez has been an unbelievable support. He was willing to risk it all to help me. Look at all we've built up through YouTube. We've spent years and years and years. Like I said, if you don't post for a few months, your YouTube journey can be over. You can lose everything.

But after my dad died, Jez phoned me and said: 'Mate, I don't care how long you need to take off. Take as long as you need. Even if it's months and months or whatever, you just take as long as you need.'

For a guy who has himself put in five years of graft to get where he is, and then to be willing to sacrifice that on my behalf, how amazing is that? I thought: 'Wow for him to do that – his morals are so strong. He's got such a code.'

He was just a perfect support to me. He was there when I needed him to be, and when I needed space he gave me space. He was just the best. So, full credit to him. Not many people at the height of their career would say: 'Mate, I'll drop it for you.' He was prepared to lose it all, just for me.

Jez: Well, it hit me hard. We were on set for the NBC show when Bill got the news. It was awful. He called me over and he could hardly talk. He just said: 'He's gone, Jez, he's gone.'

It hit me like a tonne of bricks. It was all quite sudden, but he'd been in hospital for a few weeks. It was 50/50 whether he would make it but we always believed and hoped that the best would happen, rather than the worst. So, I felt paralysed when Bill told me that. I started to cry a little bit.

I knew immediately how to respond. With what we do, it's not a job where you can go through the motions and keep your head down if you're sad. With our job, cameras are on, you're expected to be energetic, have banter and be upbeat. It's just not possible to do that if you're grieving.

Family and relationships always come first. It comes with The F2

territory that we are the face, we are the product. But we're also human, you know? People treat us like a product. Which is fine to an extent, but it can mean we're viewed almost like machines – the human element and emotion can be all taken out of it.

But we are human – both of us. That gets overlooked sometimes. If anyone understands all this it's Bill and me, we're the ones in the thick of it. So even though we spend a lot of time interacting with people who ignore the human element, we experience it with each other. We feel each other's feelings, and note the highs and lows that each of us has as human beings.

Billy: You were great.

Jez: Mate, I know you'd be exactly the same if the tables were turned.

Over the years, our friendship has actually become stronger. If you do anything that's powerful and hardcore, a bond builds up between you. That's why fighters hug each other, just after they've tried to knock each other out. They've been through something intense together.

With Bill it's the experience of a lifetime, there's just us two. So, it's natural that the friendship has grown so much stronger. We've gone along this untrodden path together. It didn't exist, that path. There's never been an F2 before. This is a new world so it's been intense!

What I do know is that we've gone on this journey together and it's made us very, very close. When his Dad died I felt like a bit of me died, too. Because his Dad really supported and encouraged us. Without him, there would be no F2 because it was him who taught young Bill how to play, pointed him in the right directions, always encouraged him, took him to watch Spurs.

All of that and so much more made Billy who he is, and who Billy is makes up 50 per cent of what The F2 is. We're both parts of the whole and therefore both parts of each other.

So, when Billy's Dad died I felt like I'd lost a part of me, because Billy had lost a part of him.

Billy: I wrote in the first book about my Dad and what he means to me. So, it was weird how it happened when he got ill. It was the day the book came out that he was rushed to hospital and then he spent five weeks in hospital before he passed away. He was under sedation for that time so he never got to read those words I wrote about him.

That was an added trauma for me, to be honest. I kept asking myself: 'Why did this happen now? Why could he not at least have been able to read my words before he went?'

So, we tried to speak the words to him a different way. My cousin Greg, who I also paid tribute to in the book, he read the whole two pages at my Dad's funeral. The vicar at the funeral had said: 'Words that were written while he was still alive will always be more powerful than words written after he passed away. Because you're not mourning someone after they passed, you're celebrating them while they're still alive.' In that way the first book, and what I wrote about my Dad, turned out to be so important.

Jez: Family is much more important than anything, isn't it? Parents are so important. I just said: 'Mate, forget about anything F2 related. I'll do my best to keep things ticking over, but even if nothing is coming out, it doesn't matter. Take time to grieve, take time to take comfort. You're the man of the family now.'

What a tough time it was. I can only imagine what Bill and his family have gone through. He could have crumbled but he came back and started making videos again.

It's a high-pressure job being in The F2. Fun, but high-pressure. You have to be 'on' all the time. You are expected to be bubbly and funny on set, no matter what is going on inside you.

I sent Bill a message a few months after it happened to say how inspired I was and am to see the strength he showed to come through it. I honestly don't know how I would be if my Dad passed away. I don't know if I'd have pushed through like he did. I didn't know what was going to happen. I didn't know if he'd be able to bounce back. Some people take years to come back. Some people never come back, but Bill's a special guy. And so was his Dad.

F2 ACADEMY: MESSI V

Billy: This is the big debate of our time, isn't it?

Jez: Dead right! I like that it has got closer between these two. I felt for a while as though Lionel Messi was way ahead, but now I feel it's closer. On overall career stats it's Messi, but on recent stats it's closer. Cristiano Ronaldo is staking his claim. Neymar is pushing closer to those two, too.

Billy: So, come on, then: who are you plumping for?

Jez: It's tough for me to call. I'd have always said Messi before but more recently I feel like Ronaldo is close.

RONALDO

Also, Messi has been in a better team overall. Messi's teams have always been based around him, which opens up different dimensions.

I would love to know if you switched teams, what would the stats look like then. If Ronaldo played for Barca and Messi played for Real – that would be the only way to know.

In the meantime, I feel like we just have to be grateful that these two all-time legends are both playing in our lifetimes.

Billy: That's it, really. Just be respectful and enjoy the show!

TEKKERS MASTERS:

ZLATAN IBRAHIMOVIC

'I'M NOT SURE ANY OTHER PLAYER QUITE HAS HIS AURA AND CHARISMA.'

Billy: Hey, Jez, did you know that when Zlatan was born he drove his Mum home from the hospital?

Jez: I heard that Zlatan does not obey the laws of gravity, they obey him.

Billy: Doesn't surprise me at all – Zlatan once killed two stones with one bird.

Jez: Ha! I love me a #ZlatanFact, because here's a man that deserves all the attention he receives.

Billy: Well, Zlatan is another one you don't want to look over and see in the tunnel, isn't he? He's not just six foot five inches tall – he's a giant in every way. As an opponent, you can prepare tactically all you like and spend ages getting yourself in the zone for the big match, but against some players that planning will only take you so far. Especially when Zlatan's on the other side.

He just has this unbelievable stature and presence. He will overturn a lot of his opponent's preparation just with his excellence alone. There's nothing you can do about that. You just have to hope, really!

Jez: Yep, yep, yep. I mean, look, there's only one Zlatan. It's just as simple as that. You're right, Billy: in terms of presence, I think he's out on his own in the modern game. If he walks into a room, everyone will feel his persona like a star exploding. I'm not sure any other player quite has his aura and charisma. He's definitely a huge personality.

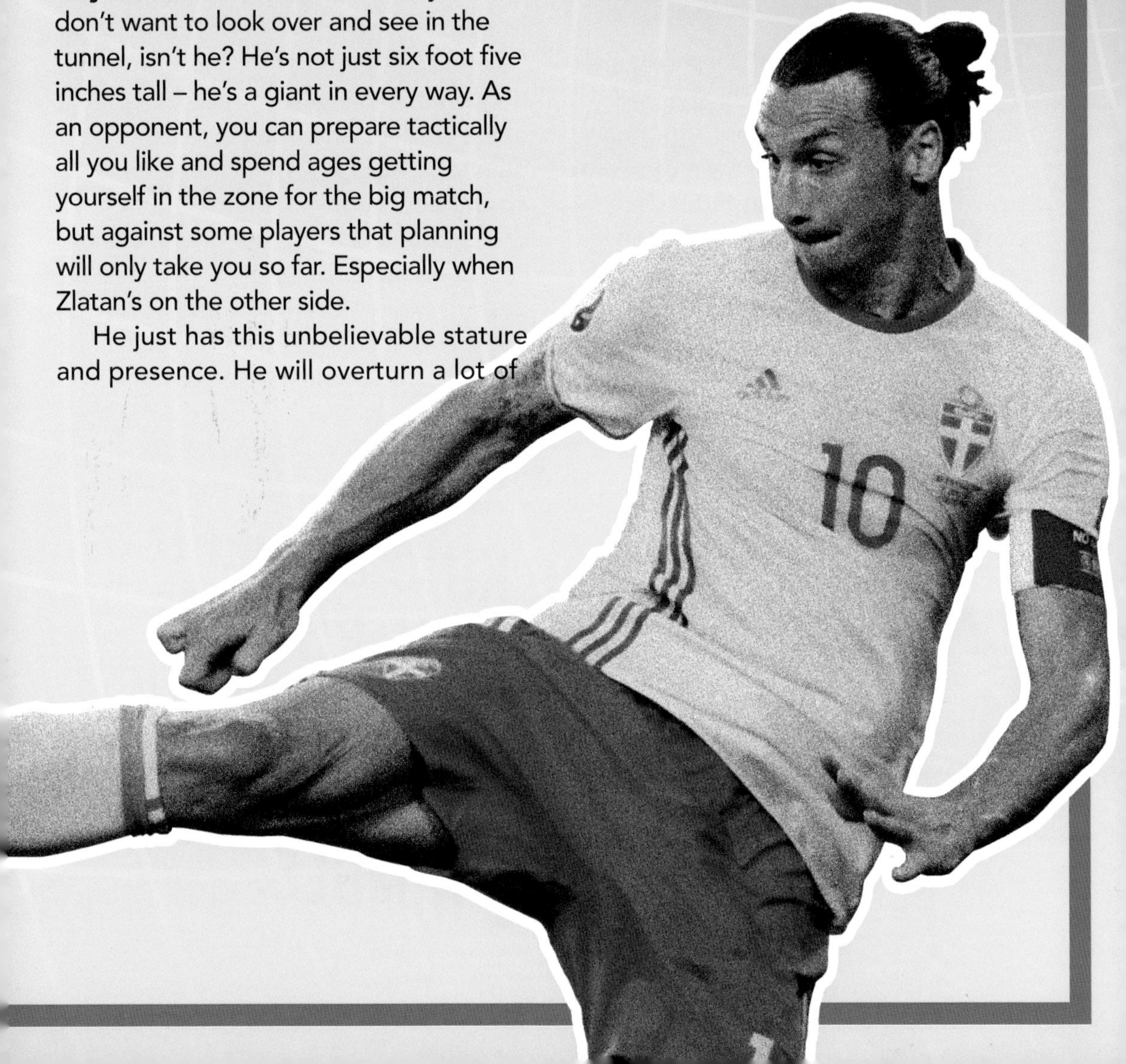

He's a bit like Eric Cantona and Paolo Di Canio, players like that. Huge self-assurance mixed with a brilliantly out-there personality. Football needs more of these characters as far as I'm concerned. There are far too many boring players and managers out there, you know. Whether it's because they've been media trained to be safe, or something else, I don't know. But there's just too many.

Billy: I've gotta say that's true. We want the exciting personalities back. I think all football fans do. It's all about entertainment, after all.

Jez: That's so right, Bill. I like players like Zlatan, Mario Balotelli and Paul Pogba; managers like José Mourinho and Jürgen Klopp. These are guys who are very controversial at times, but I love the entertainment factor they bring to the sport. It's never a dull moment with any of them.

'Cos look at the maths of it. For any club, the football itself is just 90 minutes or 180 minutes a week. That's great but, as fans, between the matches we want the game to keep entertaining us, day in, day out. So, we need the likes of Zlatan and the rest to keep the interest levels up during and – crucially – between the matches.

Look at other sports, such as F1 and boxing. I mean, I'm not saying footballers should trash-talk like boxers do, but what I am saying is that the interviews and the build-up can sometimes be more exciting than the event itself in that sport. That's down to the personalities in boxing – and Zlatan has that personality. He's not just talk, though. He backs it up on the pitch as well. He's an all-round star – truly a one-off.

Billy: Match day-wise, I think he's one of the players who doesn't need to be on the ball 24/7, because he can always pop up with that one moment of magic and win you the game. Even if he's been quiet for 70 or 80 minutes, he doesn't worry because he knows he can get that one chance and then: bang, he's won you the match or even the trophy. That's what he's been doing for years: unreal flicks, overhead kicks…

'HE KIND OF DEFIES TYPICAL PHYSICS BECAUSE HE'S SUCH A BIG GUY AND YET HE'S NIMBLE.'

Jez: Such an acrobat! I just think he's a really nice guy and an unbelievable player. He kind of defies typical physics because he's such a big guy and yet he's nimble. He's so good with his feet. You don't see that combination so much. Oftentimes players of his height can be a bit clumsy with their feet – mentioning no names, of course!

Billy: Oh go on, drop someone in it, Jezza. Spill!

Jez: I'm saying nothing, Bill. I'm not going there.

Billy: Anyway, he's quite simply a megastar, isn't he? When teams sign megastars, it gives the whole club a lift. The presence of that big name is so powerful. Imagine how United fans felt when they first saw him in their shirt. When he walked out on the pitch for them for the first time. In a level of big personalities, his stands out as probably the biggest.

Jez: Some of the stuff he's come out with over the years is unreal. He's never dull, I can tell you that. He's entertaining on the pitch and entertaining off it. Stick a mic or a tape recorder in his face and you don't quite know what's going to happen next, but you know it's going to be funny or opinionated. Good on him. Let's hope the next generation of footballers watch him and follow his example. Maybe in five years' time we'll have a league full of characters like Zlatan Ibrahimovic – that would be a dream come true, I'm rubbing my hands just thinking about it!

Billy: Me, too. Especially since I heard that Zlatan took a lie detector test – the machine confessed everything...

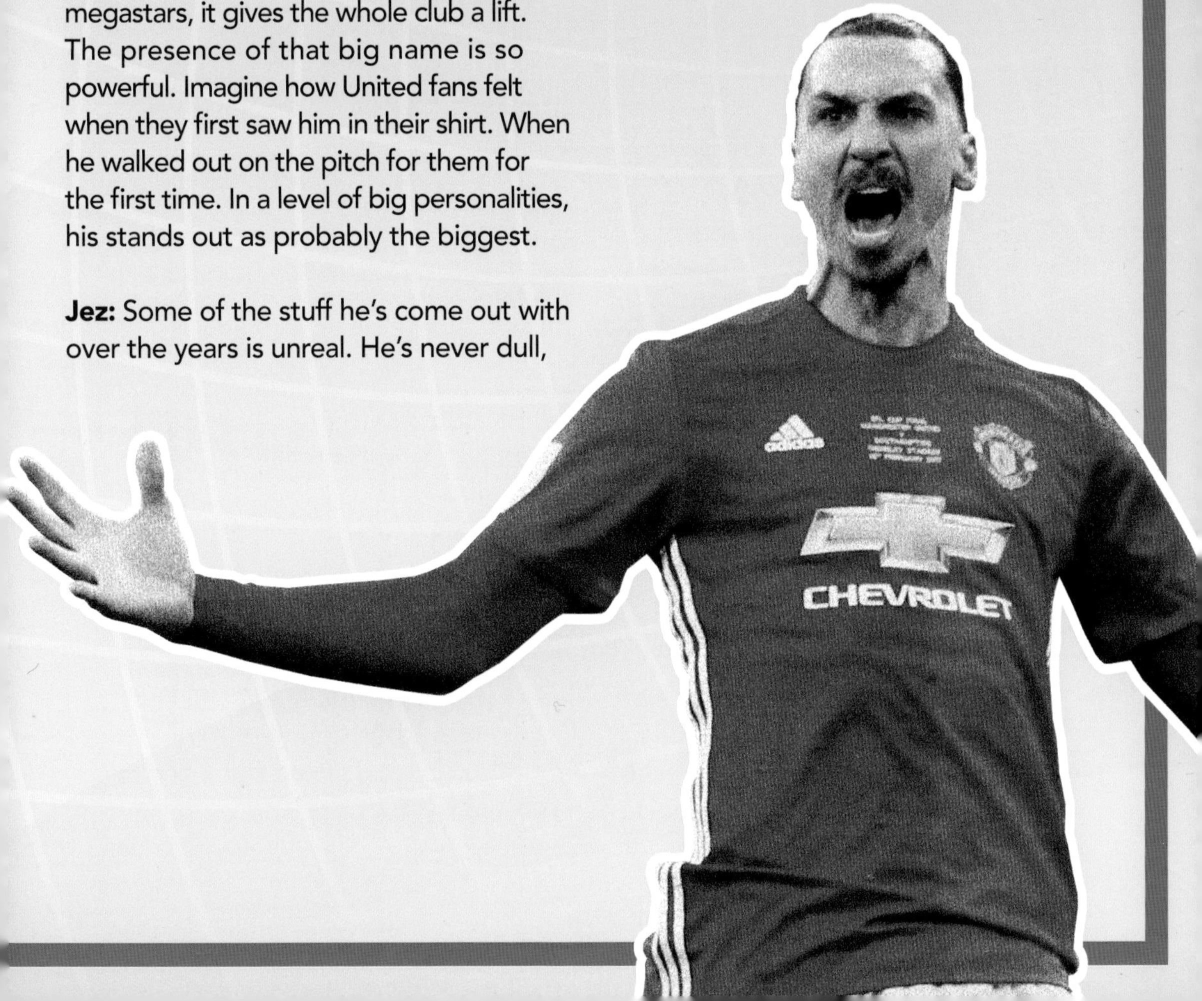

GET THE SKILLS: RONALDINHO INSTANT FIRST TOUCH

FACT FILE

ORIGIN: UNKNOWN
SKILL TYPE: CONTROL
DIFFICULTY RATING: 6
TEKKERS RATING: 8
FREQUENTLY USED BY: RONALDINHO, BERGKAMP, INIESTA

Jez: Everyone knows that one of the most important skills in football is your first touch. Master that and you're halfway to becoming a total baller and a real Tekkers master. The Ronaldinho Instant First Touch, though, is the pinnacle of all first touches. If you can perform this on a football pitch then you can probably do anything.

This skill is all about soft feet. Keep you foot floppy as the ball approaches and try to take the sting out. The perfect Instant First Touch is one that takes the flight out of the ball and leaves it in front of you ready for your next trick. Get on the pitch and give it a try, then try and perform it in a match.

LIFT YOUR HEEL AND POINT YOUR TOES DOWN AS THE BALL APPROACHES

BRING YOUR FOOT AWAY FROM THE BALL AS IT DROPS TO THE GROUND

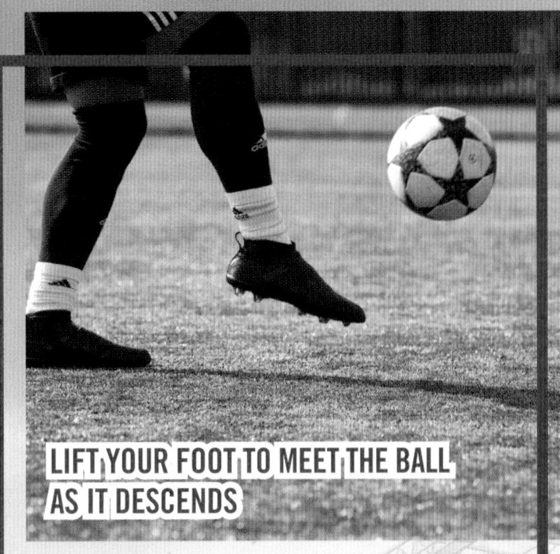

LIFT YOUR FOOT TO MEET THE BALL AS IT DESCENDS

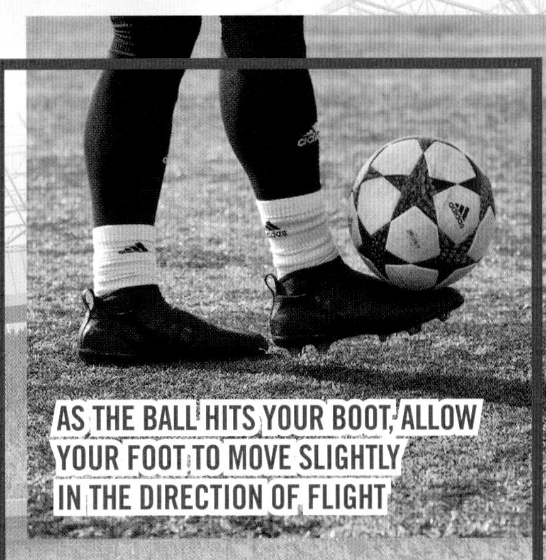

AS THE BALL HITS YOUR BOOT, ALLOW YOUR FOOT TO MOVE SLIGHTLY IN THE DIRECTION OF FLIGHT

F2
CHAPTER
SIX

adidas

PLANET F2: SUÁREZ AND MESSI!

We jetted off to Barcelona for Adidas to film with Lionel Messi and Luis Suárez. (Like you do!) The film was a bid to break the world record to control a ball from the highest height ever recorded. A ball was dropped from a crane and had to be brought under control with one touch.

Billy: The idea for this video was that we were putting the guys to the test. Fronting up to two of the best players in football history and setting them an unbelievable challenge. If you can control a ball that has been dropped from over 35 metres, then you have the world record as the highest touch ever.

First of all, it was fun just hanging out with them both. Messi was giving Suárez some banter, as well as some moral support. You'd think it would be just moral support, wouldn't you? But there was definitely a bit of banter off camera, too!

Jez: Yeah, he was, he enjoyed seeing Suárez struggle a bit, to be honest. He was entertaining himself.

Billy: Banter or no banter, Suárez managed to pluck one. Whoosh – 65mph the ball comes down. It swings from left to right. You have to watch it closely right up until the last moment. Luis gave it just the lightest touch and controlled it. Amazing.

It was so good to watch it all live. After they went, Jez and I decided that while we were in the position we would try and break the record ourselves. We both did it relatively quick, within a few minutes.

I'd actually done it the day before in rehearsals. I'd had to show Suárez's agent that it was safe and doable as a challenge. They had turned up in numbers – an entourage of about 20. Talk about pressure! I thought: don't make a mess of this, Bill. They might pull the plug on the whole thing!

LaLiga
QATAR
AIRWAYS

I focused and pulled it off. Two of them went really well. Great controls. Nice. The agent said: 'No problem, that's fine.' Phew.

When Suárez did it the next day, the ball kind of bounced off so quickly that you hardly noticed it happened. Messi tried one on his knee at one point and it just bounced right back into the air.

To make it work you have to make your foot so soft, like jelly almost. As the ball comes down, you're taking all the speed out of the ball. Trust me, though, it's so much easier said than done. To cushion the ball is just so tough. I reckon Ronaldinho would be one of the few people to do it consistently.

Also, on the practice day it had been nicer weather so it was easier. As bad luck would have it, the day of the filming itself was really windy and that only made it much harder for Luis. The ball could move 12 feet from side to side in just one drop of three or four seconds. The wind was unbelievable.

Jez: Yeah, if the ball hit you from that height it could cause some serious damage. It's proper scary. Yeah, it was really windy, man. To be fair, the wind chopped and changed. It picked up after they left. A tiny gust can cause a huge movement in the ball.

But, like Bill said, it was a joy in itself just seeing the guys again. We

got to speak to Suárez lots more than last time. We asked him about being the best striker in the world for kids coming up. We asked him loads of questions. I asked him a few about being one on one with the keeper.

He's a humble guy. It didn't take him long to pull off the trick. What a day. Ask anyone in the game or in business: time with Suárez and Messi is like gold dust.

We'll keep crossing paths and I can't wait for the next time. We should do a video with them about finishing – that would be ridiculous. It's Luis Suárez and Lionel Messi, for goodness' sake!

Billy: It was good to see Messi's 'beardage' close up, too. I'm not sure I'd be able to grow a Messi beard. Jez probably could but my beard game is not that strong, to be fair. I haven't quite got the beard tekkers. I probably would grow one if I could – a facial tribute to the legend.

They followed our lead on blond hair, dyeing their hair blond. Jez did it, then I did it as a joke. Now, it seems everyone is jumping on the old blond bandwagon. But if either of us two is going to be able to grow a Messi beard, it would be Jez.

Jez: I wouldn't necessarily be opposed to that, as it goes...

F2 ACADEMY:

THE GAFFER TAPES

JOSÉ MOURINHO

Billy: Jez, I know you're a big fan of José's style, so why don't you kick this one off?

Jez: Yeah, well I've always said that I like the true characters in football. Don't get me wrong, what matters most to fans is the silverware that a manager delivers to the club and the style of play he instils in the team. But personality counts, too, particularly for the neutrals. Watching the bosses gesticulating on the touchline is all part of the drama of the game. So are the things they say during interviews and press conferences.

It's great when you have bosses who can get a bit dramatic, a bit edgy and outrageous – and there's no boss in the English game more like that than José Mourinho.

Billy: Yeah, I get that. Let's not forget his actual achievements, though. This man has won eight league titles, two Champions Leagues and a Uefa Cup. Add in the rest, and he's won 24 trophies. All that, and he's still relatively young by managerial standards. What will he have achieved by the time he's Ferguson's or Wenger's age?

Jez: The guy is a trophy magnet. He's all about winning – you can see that by the tactics he employs. First and foremost, he wants his teams to win, and if that means they have to play more solid and cautious football, he doesn't mind.

Billy: He's got a bit of a job on his hands at Manchester United, but the fact he took that job speaks volumes in itself. After David Moyes and Louis van Gaal struggled there, a lot of coaches would have given Old Trafford the slip. But Mourinho took it on. It will be fascinating to see how his career there pans out in the years ahead.

JÜRGEN KLOPP

Jez: I like his personality a lot, I think he's a character and that's important in football. He's one of the biggest personalities in football. I like entertaining characters and it's great to have him in the Prem. Would I have him as Arsenal manager? That's a totally different story. Probably not.

Billy: His pressing game in Germany was legendary and like Jez said, his personality is a treat on its own. There are not enough gaffers like him – guys who make you stay in your seat after you've watched a game on TV. You want to see what he's going to say and how he's going to say it.

Jez: An entertainer in every sense.

F2 ACADEMY:

PEP GUARDIOLA

Jez: I love him. I'd snap him up as Arsenal manager in a second. When Arsène Wenger decides that he's going to pack it in, I want Pep. I realise he's busy at Manchester City, but I'd bring him to the Emirates without a moment's hesitation.

Billy: I doubt there's a Premier League club who wouldn't want Pep. He won 13 trophies at Barca, including three La Liga titles and two Champions League. The man is a legend.

Jez: He's stylish, too. He always looks neat, dapper and sharp. Like Bill said, who wouldn't want him?

ARSÈNE WENGER

Billy: I'm going to kick off this one because things have got so charged at Arsenal with this guy, I think I'll be able to see it a bit clearer. When you look at what he's done, it's unreal: two doubles, the Invincibles, six FA Cups.

Jez: It's also the wider work he's done – he's transformed Arsenal Football Club on and off the pitch. He's also done so much for the English game, introducing new ideas about training, preparation and diet.

Billy: That's right. Plus, Wenger has had some of the players with the most tekkers of the last 20 years: Dennis Bergkamp, Thierry Henry, Nwankwo Kanu, Robert Pires, Mesut Özil, Alexis Sánchez – the list just goes on and on. Magical players who dazzle us all.

ANTONIO CONTE

Jez: I love his passion on the touchline. It adds to the entertainment of the match. I actually thought about him when I went to the Superbowl in America. That day, it felt the whole thing was more than a game – it was an event. It was all very epic and big – he brings a dash of that to the Prem.

Billy: As a fan, you want to see things like passion on the touchline all the time in your boss. You want passion from both the manager and the players. If a manager is just sitting there on the touchline you don't know if he cares, but if someone is like Conte, you know they care. You see it.

Jez: It's visceral, you can see how it all affects him. So, I'll always favour a manager who shows emotions over one who doesn't.

TEKKERS MASTERS:

LUIS SUÁREZ

'HIS DRIVE TO SUCCEED IS OFF THE CHARTS.'

LUIS SUÁREZ

SPEED: 9
VISION: 8
TOUCH: 8
FINISHING: 10
TEKKERS: 8

F2 TRUMPS

Jez: Listen, this guy is one of the most misunderstood players in the game. A lot of people get him wrong because in the past he's done some things on the pitch that he's not best proud of but, having met him personally, I can tell you, Luis really is a sound and cool man.

Seriously, he is. During all of our personal experiences with him he has been nothing short of an absolute gentleman. Wherever I go, I sing his praises to everyone who wants to listen, because perceptions of him are unfair. He's a top, top guy.

Billy: That's right, Jez. The media seems to present him as some kind of villain because of his antics in the past. Those incidents were unfortunate, I think he'd say that himself, but they were just his passion to win going into overdrive.

When you meet Luis, you find out that he's a really calm, collected guy who is friendly. He's actually quite soft and gentle at times – bet you weren't expecting that, were you? Most people in the world don't understand this: that he's one of the nicest players you'll meet. We've met a lot, so I feel we can make that kinda call with authority. Obviously, the media have made him out to be some sort of animal – but listen, he's really not.

Jez: Okay, enough of that for now. Let's focus on the man's abilities. Talent-wise, I called it early on Suárez! When he first moved to Liverpool, everyone was raving about Andy Carroll because they both moved to Anfield at the same time. But Suárez had just come off the back of scoring 49 goals in one season for Ajax – he was the club's player of the year for the second time and the Dutch footballer of the year. He'd also scored 47 goals for the national team.

So, I called it right there – I'm not just saying this now. At the time, I said: 'Forget Andy Carroll, this Luis Suárez guy is the one to watch!' Luis had a slow start for Liverpool. Andy Carroll was the big star at first. But I continued to believe in my man, Suárez! Then, after a few months, he started delivering and now he's a household name around the world. He went on to score 69 goals in 110 appearances for Liverpool and then got his big move to Camp Nou. Before any of that happened, I remember sticking up for him and championing his ability when he wasn't being recognised so much. I was so on to that guy! I called it!

Billy: All right, all right we get the picture, Jez – you spotted him first. Can we get on with this now? Let's look back at our meetings with him. We've been lucky enough to have had two so far. Remember when we were filming with him and we set him a challenge – to get the ball into a washing machine from 22 yards?

Luis said: 'It's difficult, you know, it's a small target.' That was the first thing he said. I thought: 'Okay, maybe it's going to take him quite a few attempts to get it in. That's cool, we've got time.' But then with his first shot he got the ball straight through the hole and into the washing machine. Wow.

He just loves football. If there's a kickabout he'll play in any position you want – even in goal, diving about and loving it. He's never lost that childlike enthusiasm. There's something so pure about his attitude to the game. He's just a top, top guy and an unreal talent.

Jez: Oh, 100 per cent, 100 per cent. Right now, I actually think he's the best striker in the world. He can make a chance out of nothing – he's so unpredictable and unorthodox in the way he plays. That's what's so brilliant about him.

He's the complete striker. His heading is amazing, he's lethal inside the box and outside the box, his movement is nothing short of ridiculous. He's so intelligent: his movement off the ball is phenomenal. He's one of the best in football history, I would say. I really do rate him that highly.

Billy: I remember talking to him about how when he steps on to the pitch he is so, so desperate to win. I asked him how he keeps that drive, week in, week out, year after year – because some professionals sometimes lose that, you know. I'm not saying that critically, it's easier said than done to keep your motivation levels up over long periods of time.

So, I asked him how he manages it. He basically said that in his career he is always obsessively trying to better whatever he's done. He's got so much passion: he wants to win every 50/50 challenge, he wants to get every pass perfect, he wants to tuck away every shot. His drive to succeed is off the charts.

'HE JUST LOVES FOOTBALL. IF THERE'S A KICKABOUT HE'LL PLAY IN ANY POSITION YOU WANT – EVEN IN GOAL.'

Jez: And you know what? Sometimes opposition fans are critical of him because of various things that have happened, but if he gets linked to a club, those same fans immediately want him so bad. They are begging their club to whack the chequebook out! You want him in your side and you hate him to be on the other side. That's for a reason – his talent.

Billy: Yes. Another dimension of all this is that he lifts up the whole team. When you've got a player in your side that believes he can change the game at any moment, and who has the talent to back that belief up, it's a massive boost for the team.

Because, check this: even if you're losing in a match and the clock is ticking down, you know there's always every chance that Suárez can turn the game on its head with a moment or two of pure magic. You simply keep believing.

It's a bit like Gareth Bale at Spurs – you knew he could do something special at any moment. You never felt defeated during a match. What an asset that is.

GET THE SKILLS: LYNCH CRUYFF

FACT FILE

ORIGIN: NEW EXCLUSIVE SKILL!
INVENTED BY JEREMY LYNCH, UK
SKILL TYPE: DRIBBLE
DIFFICULTY RATING: 7
TEKKERS RATING: 8
FREQUENTLY USED BY: MR J. LYNCH

Jez: When Dutch Tekkers Master extraordinaire Johan Cruyff invented his famous turn, it shook the world of football. Cruyff died last year, and here's my tribute to the legend; the Lynch remix, if you like, with extra Jezza Jam, and a sprinkling of sweet, sweet sugar. This is a skill to get you out of a tight spot. It's useful if you're on the touchline trying to escape a close defender, or to make room for a cross.

Essentially it's a double fake. First you fake the cross, then you fake the Cruyff turn, then you spin out and accelerate away. It's bewildering, it's mesmerising, it's fast and you'd better believe it's furious. Take it, bake it and make it, my friends.

APPROACH THE DEFENDER SIDE-ON

FAKE TO HIT THE BALL

THEN FAKE TO CUT THE BALL BEHIND YOUR LEG, THEN INSTANTLY...

...TWIST OUT

TOUCH THE BALL WITH THE OUTSIDE OF YOUR BOOT...

... BACK THE WAY YOU CAME

ACCELERATE AWAY

FAKE THE CUT
TWIST
TOUCH
ACCELERATE

adidas
COUPE DE

F2
CHAPTER
SEVEN
adidas

PLANET F2: MAURICIO POCHETTINO

We filmed with Spurs gaffer Pochettino at the Tottenham training ground. The video was a creative of him putting us two through various sets of skills and rating them out of 10. There were some great viral pieces from the video and we found that Pochettino had great tekkers.

Jez: You know, one of the biggest questions people ask us is: 'Can you really play? Are you the real deal?'

So, this shoot was a good chance to test ourselves under pressure. Our tekkers was bang on form. He was impressed with us and we got our skills certified by one of the best managers in the game.

Billy: We did. A few weeks after the shoot I was in Nando's, and I actually bumped into someone who knows Poch. He said he had been round at Pochettino's house and they had chatted about our video with him. Poch told him two awesome things:

One – he told him that after the filming he couldn't move properly for 10 days because that was the most activity he'd done for a while. Ha, ha!

Two – he said that if we'd been 10 years younger, then he would have signed us up for Spurs. Incredible. What a nice guy to say it and what a buzz for us. A real icing on the cake for the both of us, particularly me as a Spurs fan.

Obviously, age is against us now, but to know we've got the ability there is a buzz. Don't get me wrong: even if I could, I would never go back in time and risk what we've done with The F2. It's been a dream. But I stopped playing at 19 years of age. I was getting spotted by pro clubs at the time and I feel like I didn't even get near to my ability.

Jez: For Bill, I think it was an even bigger deal. Poch is probably the best Spurs manager ever. It was nice to see those two having banter. They were hugging, having a laugh at my expense

as an Arsenal fan. That right there, that would be like me and Arsène Wenger having a laugh. It blows my mind to even think about it. I was so happy for Bill to have that experience.

Poch was amazing. When we had lunch with the Spurs team that day, he told the entire coaching staff to not start eating until we got there. That's class, isn't it? You don't expect that.

Listen, Spurs is big. It's like an empire. And the guy who is at the helm of it all still conducts himself with that much class. That level of respect is amazing. He's the boss, we're the ones in awe, so him waiting for us is an experience that is hard to even describe. It's like true humility. I'm not even a Spurs fan but I've got so much respect for him. The club is under him, so while he's the manager you have to respect Spurs. Even as a Gooner!

It's clear that it's really important to him as a man how he treats others. He was talking about this at the table, actually. How important it is to get your treatment of others right. He psychoanalyses every player. He has a proper system to understand how players are feeling and how he should deal with them.

He's not just about football, tactics and training. He also wants to talk with the players about how they are feeling. How do they feel about life? Are they okay? Are they feeling homesick? Is there anything that can be changed that will help get the best out of them?

He was talking to us about how important it is that players are made to feel happy and respected. He does it with the players who aren't starting matches just as much. It makes everyone feel valued.

You can see the results on the pitch! Everyone is happy and when you watch them play, they genuinely seem motivated and energised. All of that is coming from him.

Billy: I think he's incredible, I really do. The way he isn't afraid to give young people an opportunity. There are so many people now who would rather bring in a big-money player than give younger players a go, whereas he's not afraid to give youth a chance.

Look at it: he brought on Harry Winks in the Champions League. He also brought him on against Liverpool and Manchester United. This is a young player with massive potential for sure, but he's not proven on that stage.

But Poch will put him in games that are really important because he believes he can deliver. Not many managers have that belief in the youth. Players usually have to keep proving themselves before they get that chance against the big teams. But he's not afraid to do it – which I love about him. Full credit to him for his approach.

And he's so technical and tactical about the game. Like Jez said, when we had lunch with him that day he was telling us he has psychoanalysis on every single player. He monitors them so closely that he knows how they are going to respond to certain circumstances on and off the pitch.

So, if one of the players splits up with his wife, say, Poch will know how that will affect him on the pitch and for how long. Or if a player has a car accident but isn't physically injured, Poch will know whether the experience will affect them on the pitch or not. All from the psychoanalysis programme. The same if they're having trouble selling their house or if they've had a row with their girlfriend. The manager and the club will know how it will affect them going forward. Same if the crowd are getting on a player's back – for this player will it motivate him or destroy him?

Poch will sit back and use all this intelligence to tailor his response to any problem with the individual player. He might give one player a day off to play golf or go to a spa, but then a different player with the same problem he might work them a bit harder at training. He'll tell another: 'I don't want you moping – I need you to step up.' He knows what each guy needs – the best way for each player to get them back on their game.

Jez: Make no mistake: Spurs are right in the mix for honours under Poch. Before, they were on a slightly lower tier. You wouldn't expect them to be in the Champions League and even chasing for titles, like they are now. They've shaken right off that old mentality they used to have. In the past, if they went behind they would have imploded. But not now.

Billy: Even the setbacks have good points. I think as Spurs fans we can take a positive from the fact that we didn't finish above Arsenal in the 2015/16 season, because you have to learn as a footballer and sometimes a setback is the best way of doing that. If you're a young team, like that Spurs team, you can't have it all right away. It's how you respond to the setbacks that makes you the player you will become. Football is a learning curve.

What about that 2-2 draw against Chelsea right near the end of the season? I was there. Because the game meant so much to us, we lost our heads, even though we were dominating the game. That's the learning curve – the young players can grow strength from that. That's part of learning as a pro player – these things happen. That Chelsea game was terrible but the players are young and they'll learn from it.

Jez and I both often wonder what could have been for us as pros in mainstream football. I was skilled but I wasn't strong and big. I think at 19 I was still a boy, really; I wasn't yet a man. I wonder if I'd stuck at it, how far up the league I could have gone? I only really played two seasons in semi-pro football, but in my first season I scored 17 goals. That was from left midfield. I got put in a Ryman representative team.

So, I was doing well and I do wonder what could have happened. After Pochettino said all he said, I can't help wondering what might have been.

Jez: Yeah, and I think Poch has answered that question people ask us about whether we can really play.

Billy: Final word: I was really nervous when we met Pochettino. Not because I thought he'd be a hard, harsh type, more because I am a fan. As a Spurs fan I was nervous from that respect – just meeting the guy and being able to play football with him. I can't believe this crazy life we've made for ourselves – it's top.

F2 ACADEMY: SCIENCE OF SWAZ 2

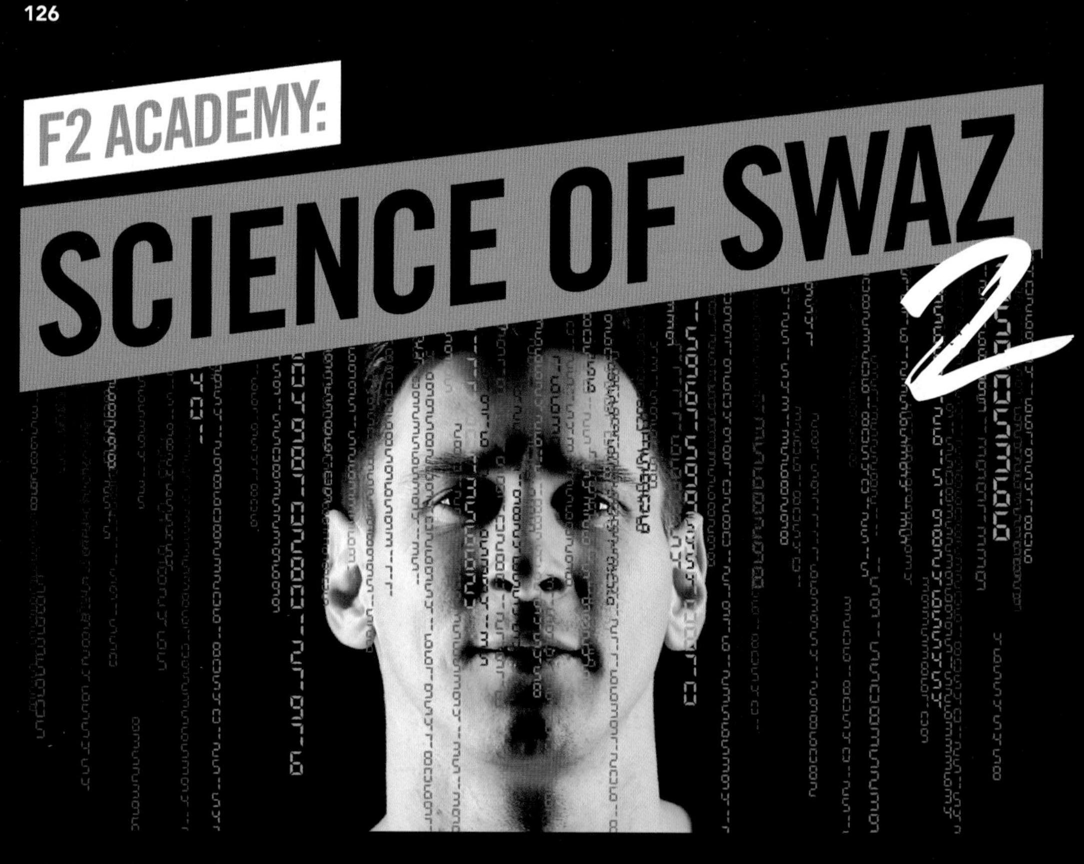

DRIBBLING

Jez: I think that the best dribblers have got that knack of looking at things other than the ball when they dribble, yet still keeping close control of the ball. It's a tricky combination to pull off but if you can master it, then you are going to destroy your opponents.

If you can look up, then you can see what's going on with your cover. You need to be aware of it and to be able to process it. So, you need to become a bit like Neo in *The Matrix*. You need to see things that others can't see.

Take Lionel Messi: he is seeing things like Neo in *The Matrix*. To everyone else, it's all happening so fast – he's beating his defenders and powering along. But to Messi, things are happening slower than they are in reality because he's become a master of processing what is happening outside of his feet.

On the other side, if you're not aware of what is going on about you, your opponents will totally spot that. Then they've got the upper hand. They know that you're playing almost half blind, which is no good for you but a whole load of good for them.

Sometimes, players only master this side of dribbling as they mature. Someone like Alex Oxlade-Chamberlain has improved a lot in this regard over the last season. He's looking up more, he's seeing more and therefore his runs are becoming more incisive. So, work on that.

DRIBBLING: THE SCIENCE OF RONALDO

Billy: This guy has got fast feet, there's no doubt about that. Everyone knows it. Not least the hundreds of opponents he's left on their backsides. But a science study showed that what was going on in his mind was also important – what he was looking at.

Although he looked at the ball a fair amount, he also looked at his opponent and into space, scanning the area for space beyond the defender. They noticed that Ronaldo made 13 moves in eight seconds – spins, step-overs: the works.

They also tracked that he was watching his opponent, noticing the angles and movement of his feet and hips to predict his next move.

Most important, though, is that he has studied hard. Keep training, guys!

POWER

Billy: The sledgehammer shot is great to get real power behind the ball. The good thing about it is that you don't have to have big muscles or strong legs, if you practise hard you can do it, whatever your build.

I normally take around four steps back, but go with what makes you feel comfortable.

Start slightly off centre. Run up with speed and power. You can strike the ball from the laces area for the best effect.

Follow through in the centre of the ball. Smash straight through it – give it some welly! Concentrate on the run-up and how you hit the ball as you train. Once the technique is mastered, you can add more power.

TEKKERS MASTERS: PAUL POGBA

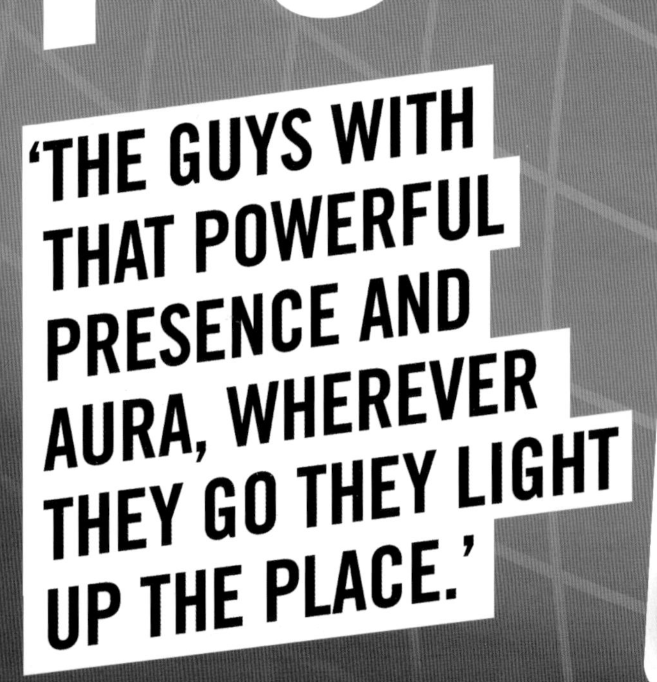

'THE GUYS WITH THAT POWERFUL PRESENCE AND AURA, WHEREVER THEY GO THEY LIGHT UP THE PLACE.'

Jez: Okay, okay… Paul Pogba is an amazing footballer. There's no disputing that and everyone already knows it. So, listen, let's come to his skills in a bit. First, let's just acknowledge this guy's amazing personality. Let's start with the pure star quality of the man!

Billy: Good shout, Jez. Let's kick things off by looking at his character. To make a successful football team you need a blend that includes a few massive personalities in the team – the sort of guys where what they do off the pitch is almost as important as what they do on it. The guys with that powerful presence and aura, wherever they go they light up the place.

Paul Pogba is very much that guy. I mean, I like the way that he's so serious on the pitch – so focused on

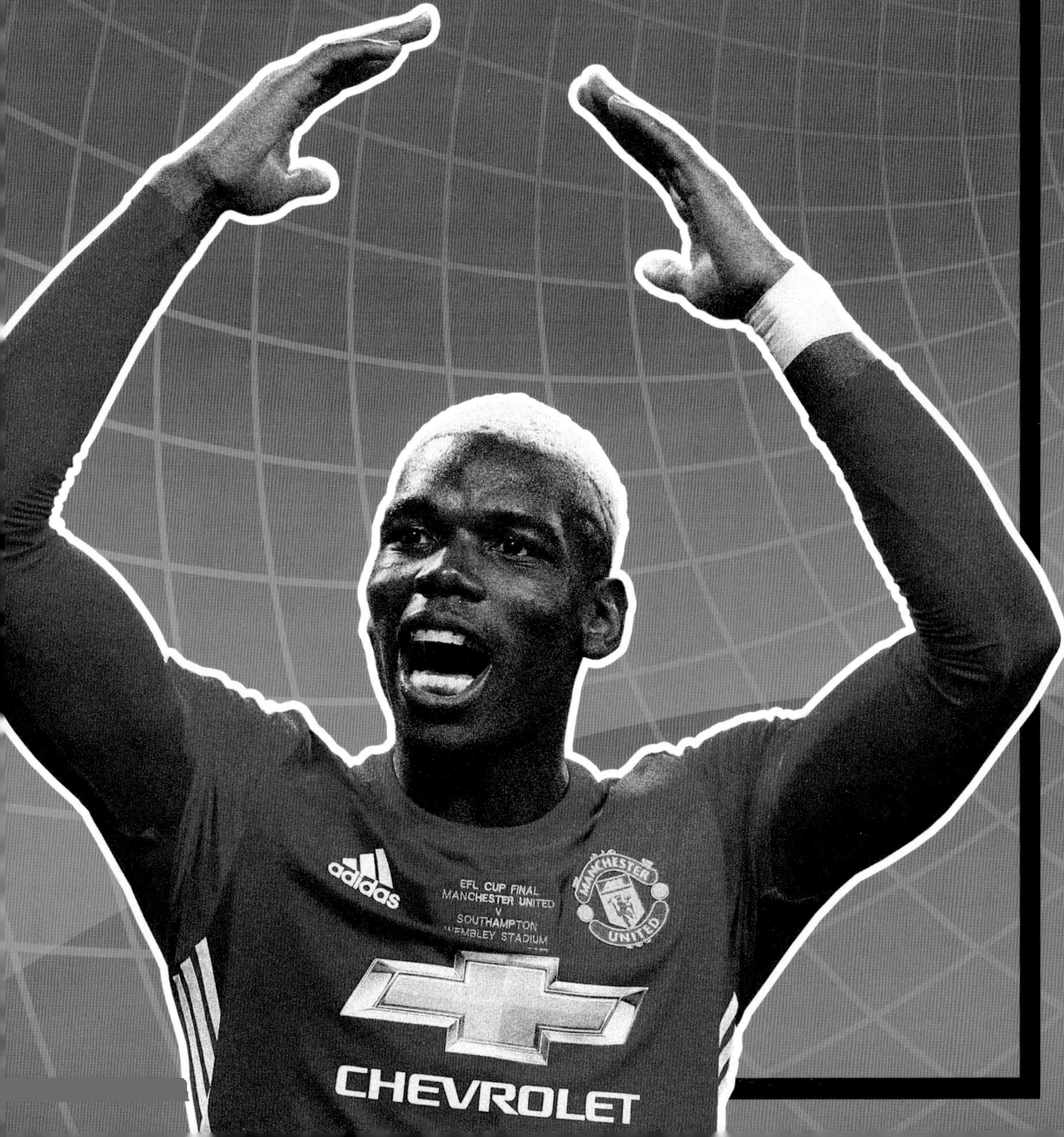

'ON THE PITCH, HE CONTROLS THE TEMPO OF THE GAME AND IT ALL RUNS THROUGH HIM.'

playing and winning. But he can break right out of that and show that he's a happy, joyful character. Off the pitch he doesn't take himself too seriously, does he? He's a humble guy and a fun-loving bloke. You can see that he's such a nice guy. Every team needs a player and character like Pogba.

Jez: That's it. He likes having fun and a laugh. He's creative. He enjoys dipping into all the extra-curricular stuff that opens up for top players. Not everyone does enjoy that, but Pogba does. He's requested to film with us and we can't wait to do it. Every time that happens it really surprises us – in such a nice way! What a buzz it will be to film with Pogba. I'm excited just thinking about it.

Billy: The other thing about Paul that is incredible is this: imagine if you're lining up against him in the tunnel before the match. You're standing there, trying to get focused for the game, and then you look over and see him. You've already lost the battle right there. You'd see his size, his stature and strength, the coolness that he oozes. You'd know he's going to go out and do what he does.

Jez: It's such a forceful charisma he's got, he's going to make you die a bit inside when you see him in the tunnel, for sure. The top players in history have had that about them, think of Roy Keane, Patrick Vieira, Eric Cantona – they could psych you out before the game's started. And they knew it, too!

Billy: On the pitch, he controls the tempo of the game and it all runs through him. Tempo is important, you see. Some teams play fast, some teams play slow. But Pogba can dictate at what tempo the game is played out. He can just switch it at any moment – bang! He's so intelligent. He'll slow the game down and then just when the opponents feel steady, all of a sudden he'll launch a super-fast counterattack.

Although he mainly plays as a central midfielder, he's also a potent force out there on the left, or in a holding role, or in a more attacking role. He can do it all. He will pull unexpected stuff out of the bag sometimes. He's just a nightmare to play against and a dream to play with.

And he's still so young, he's only 24. Imagine what lies ahead for this guy? All the trophies he's going to win and how much he will improve. It's scary just to think about it.

Some people would have been crushed if they'd had an experience with a club like he had when he left Manchester United – it wasn't the most friendly departure and even Sir Alex Ferguson was a bit 'good riddance' about it all. But he went on to win Serie A titles with Juventus, he made a Champions League final appearance and also won a chunk of personal honours, popping up in selections for team of the year and player of the tournament. Then he went back to Manchester United for something like

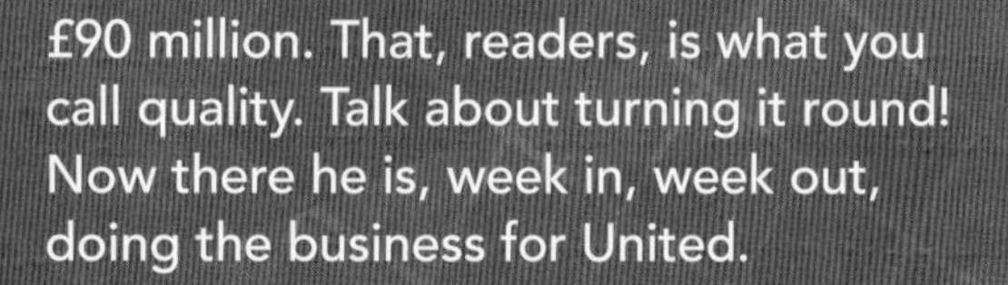

£90 million. That, readers, is what you call quality. Talk about turning it round! Now there he is, week in, week out, doing the business for United.

Jez: Years ago, there were so many players who played his sort of role, but nowadays there aren't quite so many about. He's integral to Manchester United. He can do the lot. Pogba is a jewel in every way – just the sort of man we like to see in the game. A stunner of a talent, a top guy and just a superstar all round. He's had some pretty decent haircuts, too. Check out some of his chops on Google Images!

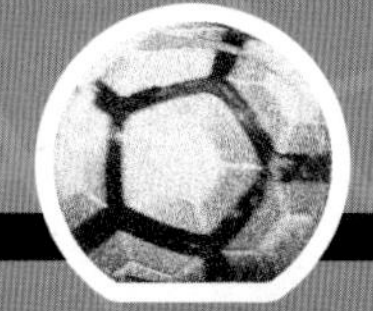

GET THE SKILLS: SCORPION KICK

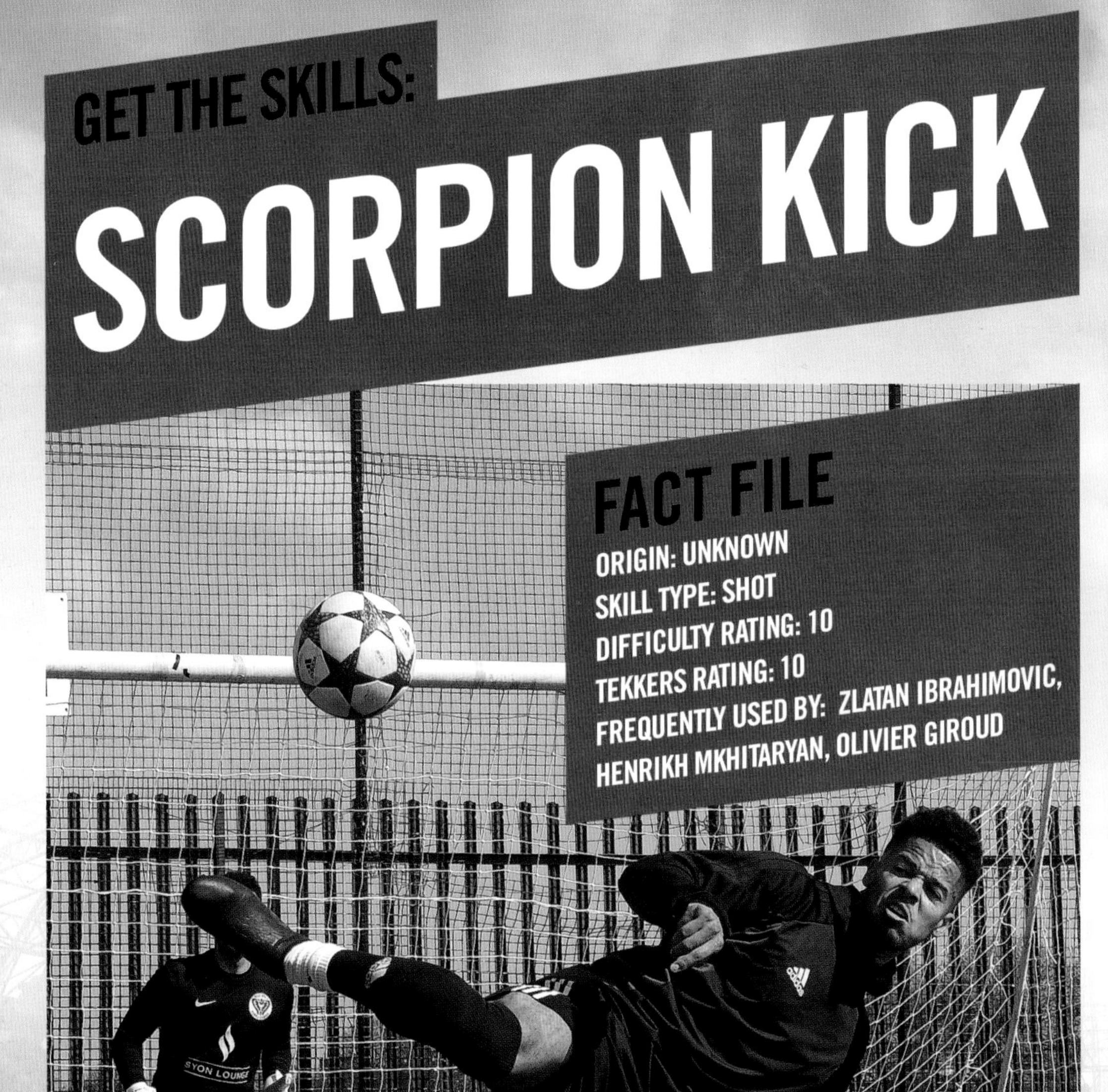

FACT FILE

ORIGIN: UNKNOWN
SKILL TYPE: SHOT
DIFFICULTY RATING: 10
TEKKERS RATING: 10
FREQUENTLY USED BY: ZLATAN IBRAHIMOVIC, HENRIKH MKHITARYAN, OLIVIER GIROUD

Jez: Something must have happened in the last twelve months because suddenly everyone started going Scorpion Kick crazy. First Henrikh Mkhitaryan scored one on the dive for Manchester United, and then the big man, Oliver Giroud, knocked one in for Arsenal, and people were talking about 'goal of the season'. Naturally, we had to get in on the act. It's just such a beautiful thing when this goes right.

Here's how it works: first, the delivery has to be spot on. Then you need to position yourself facing where the ball is coming from, side on to the goal. As the delivery drops over your shoulder you need to twist your standing foot to face the goal at the same time as lifting your leg behind you and flicking the heel up to create that scorpion shape. It's the heel that connects with the ball. It's all about making that connection as sweet as possible – the speed and surprise will leave the keeper stranded.

LET THE DELIVERY DROP OVER YOUR SHOULDER

LEAN FORWARD AND FLICK YOUR LEG UP BEHIND YOU

START TO TURN TOWARDS GOAL

CONNECT AS SWEETLY AS YOU CAN

THE DELIVERY NEEDS TO BE SPOT ON

MOVE YOUR FEET TO GET INTO POSITION…

…TO LET THE BALL DROP OVER YOUR SHOULDER

LEAN FORWARD AND FLICK YOUR HEEL
BOSH!
CONTROL AND SPRINT AWAY

CHAPTER
EIGHT

PLANET F2: BOOK TOUR & F2 SHOW

When our first-ever book was published, we toured the UK to meet you guys: we went to Glasgow, Gateshead, Manchester, Birmingham, London and Bluewater. So many of The F2 family turned out to meet us. We also had The F2 Show, with Adidas creating a cool urban space in White City for The F2 to host our own event.

Billy: When our first book came out and we set off on a book-signing tour, that right there was when I realised the power of The F2 family. When we first discussed the idea of doing tour dates, my main concern in the meeting was that we mustn't arrange to film the tour because it will be embarrassing. I thought a maximum of 50 people would turn up and the videos would look a bit tragic.

How wrong I was. We sold out of every single tour date – 5,000-plus people turning up. So, it really hit home how many people are with us every step of the way. I was taken aback. I genuinely wasn't expecting it. You guys reading this – you're the best.

At Bluewater, we were their biggest book-signing of the year and that was some statement. They will have had some massive people there to sign books but we were the biggest of 2016. The crowds blew us away – people wearing Rascal or Adidas. It just goes to show how big The F2 family is. Maybe I'll get a tattoo about The F2 family next?

Jez: Record-breaking numbers – we felt humbled by it. The queue was so long and the kids were so patient. We were taking a bit of time with each kid, rather than rushing them through. So, at the back, they started to get a little agitated. Complaining a bit about the waiting time, but once they realised we were giving each kid a proper experience rather than just signing their books, I think the parents got it. That's a memory there, a life moment

adidas

that their kids can remember for ever. The parents all said in the end that the wait was well worth it. It was nice to have the agitated ones turn and understand what we were doing.

Billy: What we tried to do was spend at least a minute, to a minute and a half, talking to every single person. We didn't want to just sign their book and say: 'See ya later!' We wanted to chat with them, ask them about themselves. Do a picture if they wanted one. Not one person left that signing without a photo and conversation with us. And we massively appreciated the gifts: some brought us cakes and doughnuts and letters!

Fans are particularly important to us. If you're an actor you can make it without fans, even if you're a singer you can make it without fans. But for us, what we do is all about the fans. Without you guys clicking on our videos, we are nothing. So, we really, really appreciate you all.

The funny thing is that after my Dad, everything that happened last year was a blur. But let's focus on the positives. For the book to sell so well is unbelievable. Look at what we did in a year – more exciting stuff than we might have otherwise done in a whole lifetime.

Jez: We felt humbled by it all. The queue was so long and the kids were so patient. My wrist was well tired afterwards. It's a funny one – it's human nature to want a little 15-minute break, but if you take that break, there are hundreds of people waiting out there. That's a lot of man hours that you are costing everyone. The one time that we did have a five-minute break we ended up feeling guilty.

I never really expected to achieve a book tour in my life. I remember seeing a huge queue outside Waterstones when JK Rowling, the Harry Potter author, was doing one. I never ever thought that the day would come when I would be the person at the front, signing the books.

Then we had the Westfield experience. Adidas invested a million pounds into making us a pitch on the rooftops and building the other attractions. That was a first for us and for the brand, I think. For us it was a privilege that Adidas had that faith in us. We did some demos of tekkers live. The tickets were snapped up fast. We got to connect with our fans more. We want to connect more!

F2 ACADEMY: TALKING TACTICS

WHAT IS GEGENPRESSING?

Billy: Jürgen Klopp says that the best time to win the ball back is immediately after your team has lost. This is because in that moment, your opponent will be recovering from the energy of winning it back and looking around for where to take the ball next.

So, with this tactic, a team pushes high up the pitch and systematically hunts down the ball, using the principle above. But the only way this will work is if the team unit is compact. You can't leave gaps. So, if your team is practising, focus on not allowing any openings for the other side to send passes through.

WHAT IS A FALSE 9?

Jez: The best way to understand this role is as a decoy: the false 9 is a centre forward in a side without a centre forward. Confused? Well, this lone forward will drop deep at every chance. This way he can dodge markers and link up the play. So, defenders don't know how to handle him. The false 9 is not the same as the number 10, who is usually a second striker. Lionel Messi has often played as a false nine, so has Alexis Sánchez.

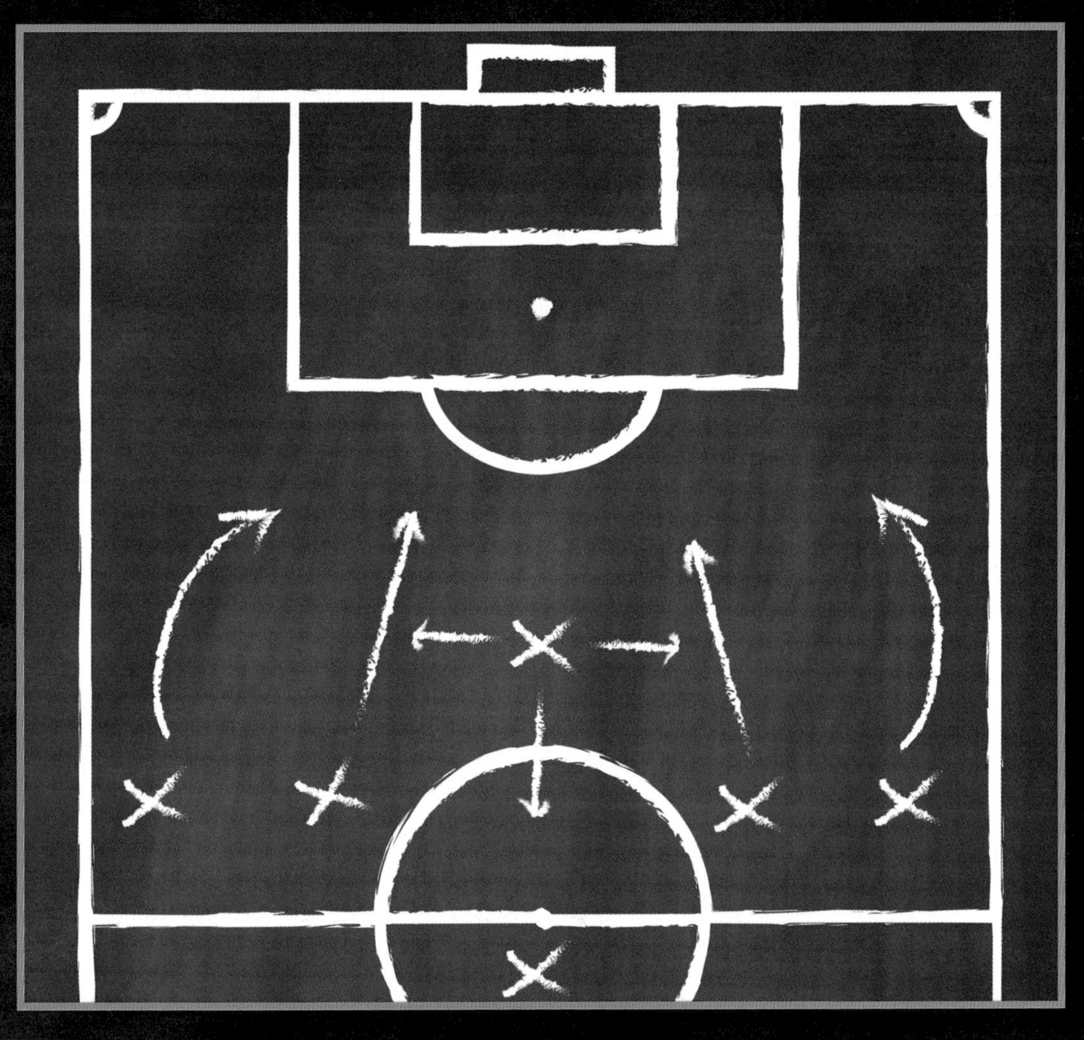

WHAT IS ZONAL MARKING?

Billy: Bill: Zonal marking is a little easier to understand – it does what it says on the tin. A good way to use it is when you are defending a corner kick. Imagine the penalty area is divided into sections, with players on the defending team responsible for one of these sections. If every guy protects his section well, you should keep a clean sheet. It's easier said than done, though!

WHAT DOES READING THE GAME MEAN?

Jez: Right now, you are reading a book about football. Does that mean you are currently reading the game? Well, not quite. Here's an easier way to get your head around this term: when you watch or play football, do you often find that you guess what is about to happen during a move? If so, then you have just read the game. This means you have a high degree of tactical sophistication. Nice one!

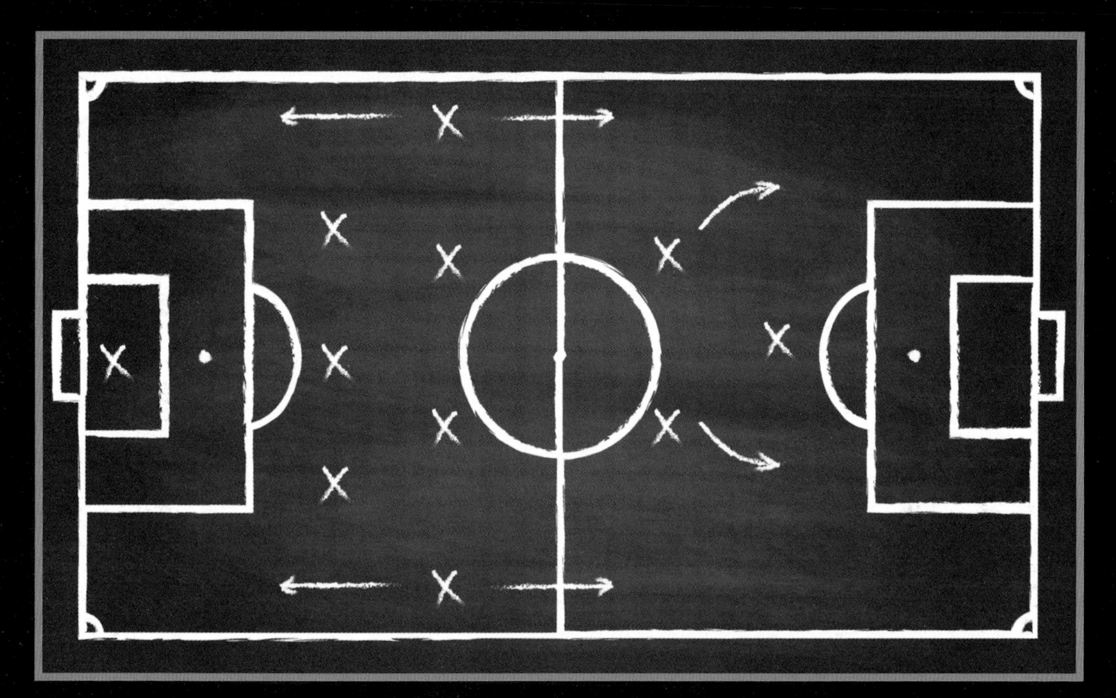

WHAT IS A 3-4-3?

Billy: When you look at Chelsea's success during the 2016/17 season, a lot of it is credited to Antonio Conte's belief in the 3-4-3 formation. But what are its strengths and weaknesses?

STRENGTHS

- Attackers can challenge full backs.
- Midfielders and attackers can constantly trade position – a nightmare for defenders!
- The four-man midfield offers width.
- The defence is particularly strong centrally.

WEAKNESSES

- The back three is vulnerable on the flanks and to sudden switches in play.
- Unless the midfielders and forwards are well drilled, they can confuse their own team-mates as much as they can bamboozle the opposition.

TEKKERS MASTERS:

KEVIN DE BRUYNE

'HE'S JUST GOT SO, SO MUCH IN HIS TOOLBOX: A WIDE RANGE OF PASSING, HE CAN SHOOT FROM ALL RANGES, DRIBBLING SKILLS.'

Billy: He's just unbelievable, isn't he? What a player. I must admit, he kind of crept up on me a bit, I wasn't that aware of him for a while but we all know about him now. He seems to have really come into his own recently.

Jez: Yeah, I'm the same. It was all a bit out of the blue, wasn't it? He kind of burst on to the scene from nowhere, even though he'd played for Genk, Werder Bremen and VfL Wolfsburg. He'd even played for the Belgian national team before he joined Manchester City. Somehow I didn't notice him so much, though.

But we all know his name now – he's made such a statement in the game. Given the chance, any top club in the world would want to sign Kevin De Bruyne. I reckon he's one of the best advanced-playmakers around. He's just got so, so much in his toolbox: a wide range of passing, he can shoot from all ranges and superb dribbling skills.

He's more than lived up to that big deal that took him to City. He really has, and there's something big I want to say right here, because his story should inspire everyone wanting to make it in the beautiful game of football. He was discarded by Chelsea after making just three Premier League appearances in two-and-a-half seasons at Stamford Bridge. Imagine how frustrating that time was for him and how hurt he must have felt when they sold him. Then, a while later, he moves to Manchester City in a big money transfer, returning to the Prem as one of Europe's elite players.

'GUARDIOLA SAYS DE BRUYNE IS ONE OF THE VERY BEST PLAYERS HE'S WORKED WITH.'

Billy: He seems kind of unique, too. I don't even know if I can compare him to another player. Who is out there like him? He's technically amazing, his intelligence is brilliant, and his football brain is unbelievable. He always seems to pick the right passes. When he gets the ball you fully expect him to do something good with it and he very rarely lets you down. What's not to like, mate?

For me, if you want an attacking player in your side, this is the one to go for. He's got it all. When we filmed with him he hit a knuckleball and got it in the net first time. He did it like it was nothing. So much poise and self-belief.

Jez: Yeah, he taught himself to do that knuckleball free kick with top-spin. He told us it took him two years to learn. Bill and me both tried it and we couldn't nail it. He could though! I guess sometimes you just need to hold your hands up.

It's not just his talent on the pitch that stands out for me, it's also his nature and personality. We've been lucky enough to get to know him a bit, but even before that we could tell he was a sound guy. You just watch him going about his work and you can see it –

he's really nice. He's one of those quiet and reserved guys. He does his talking on the pitch, for sure.

Billy: Yeah, he's got that shy character, hasn't he? Some players with his talent are so sure of themselves and you can't always blame them for that. But he's really calm and quiet. He's a bit like Mesut Özil in that way: it's when he steps on to the pitch, that's when he expresses himself. Messi is similar in a way, too. Like Jez said, these guys do their talking on the pitch. They're a bit introverted, but probably every team needs a quiet man to balance off all the bigger, more outgoing guys. It's all about balance in a team unit, after all.

He's humble, too. Kevin is a truly unbelievable player – but I don't even know if he realises how good he is. Maybe it's that humility which keeps him grounded and focused. But, however humble he is about himself, the rest of us can see his talent.

Pep Guardiola says De Bruyne is one of the very best players he has ever worked with. When you think of the talent that boss has managed, that is the most amazing compliment. Pep's moved him to a more central role recently, both in terms of his position in the starting line-up and his importance in the team. The results have been stunning. I think this is because one of his best assets is his ability to understand and find space on the pitch. Even in the biggest games, against the more terrier-like opponents, you'll see him suddenly pop up in acres of space. How did he even find that space? What a brain, what a talent and what a player.

Jez: We love him. Can't wait to work with him again.

GET THE SKILLS: SLEDGEHAMMER

FACT FILE

ORIGIN: UNKNOWN
SKILL TYPE: SHOT
DIFFICULTY RATING: 7
TEKKERS RATING: 8
FREQUENTLY USED BY: NEMANJA MATIC, DAVID LUIZ, PAUL SCHOLES, DAVID BECKHAM

Billy: A thunder-blaster, a net-buster, a pile-driver. It doesn't matter what you call it – nothing beats an absolute firebolt smashed top bins. The raw power, the connection, the keeper stranded; it's a moment of pure beauty. But here's the secret that no one tells you: it's not about muscles and trying to hit the ball as hard as you can. It's all about technique.

1: Your run up should be off-centre, a few steps, whatever's comfortable. 2: Accelerate at speed. 3: Whip your foot through the ball, striking it with the hardest, flattest bone, which is just where your laces are, driving through the centre of the ball. 4: Lean forward and follow-through with both legs off the ground and your striking boot landing first. 5: Watch the keeper pick it out of the net. That's all. Oh yeah, and mine's called the Sledgehammer.

F2
RUN UP OFF-CENTRE
PLANT YOUR FOOT NEXT TO THE BALL
HIT THE BALL ON YOUR LACES
STRIKE THROUGH THE CENTRE OF THE BALL WITH ALL YOUR MOMENTUM

RUN UP AT SPEED

LEAN FORWARD, KEEP YOUR WEIGHT OVER THE BALL

1
FOLLOW THROUGH THE CENTRE OF THE BALL
LAND STRIKING FOOT FIRST
1
LEAVE THE KEEPER STRANDED

F2
CHAPTER
NINE

We've spent a lot of time in America. We filmed with Odell Beckham Jr, the NFL's hottest and most well-known athlete currently in the sport, and also shot an NBC USA series, It's Called Football *that was shown on Boxing Day. Then we chipped off to LA for two months to film more content for our own YouTube channel and create an American series called* The F2 Go to Hollywood.

Billy: We love America. When we got the opportunity to come out to LA and film a series out here we snapped it up. Initially the idea was to film in the UK. But part of my injury had come from aggressively using my foot in cold weather, so I wasn't keen.

With proper football, when you kick the ball you're also running around the pitch. So, you're hot, warmed-up. With the filming we do, you're not hot. You're standing around, waiting for cameras to be set up. So, when we're back home it's really cold in the winter and once you're cold you can't warm up. That means you do a lot of shivering, but it also means you're more prone to injuries.

The idea was that we'd film over in LA for several months. It's been an amazing opportunity. Half the time we were there we were filming a television show called *The F2 Go to Hollywood* – it's been such a good experience.

We've also just been living the LA life. Going to the Oscars, helicopter rides, getting tickets to the Superbowl. We're having so much fun, I can't even tell you.

People say we're lucky and that we're living the life. It's true, we are having a wonderful time. But the message I want to give is that if you give it your all and you work as hard as you possibly can, you'll reap the rewards at the end. Yes, we are lucky, but we've put years of graft into what we do. We're basically enjoying the pay-off of all the hard work. It's a privileged position, but the hard work and graft has been put in.

adidas

So, the big takeaway I want to offer readers is this: do your best, go the extra mile and put the sweat in. You'll be surprised how far that can take you. Sacrifice.

I had a lovely house in LA. My family was there. My daughter was home-schooled and she also got to experience a totally new culture and lifestyle. She learned about America, learned about the world. Those months she spent out there will be memories for life. We had a lovely swimming pool and a Jacuzzi in the garden. We were literally two minutes from Beverly Hills. It was just incredible.

I can't even do it justice, the life we got to live out there. It really was living the dream. That's what it was. We went and played football with Rod Stewart in his garden one night!

I even flew my Mum out there for the last 11 days. It was a touch bittersweet because she and my Dad used to love their holidays. But I knew she could do with the experience so she came out to join us. My in-laws came out, too. We had two spare bedrooms and two spare beds, so it was really an open house for anyone we knew.

I love it. I'd move permanently over to LA in a second if I could. It's not so much the celebrities that I like, it's more about the lifestyle. It's such a steady pace. The weather's good, which makes you feel good when you wake up in the morning.

Plus, to be able to film on a pitch with sunshine and perfect temperature was great for us, particularly after our injuries. Funnily enough, though, you need a filming permit out in LA. It's thousands of pounds just to get that. Back home we pay just £12 an hour for the pitch compared to thousands of pounds a day.

Jez: Bill has said it all, man. The weather was unbelievable. It's too cold in England. We film a lot wherever we are and it's not easy in low temperatures. There's little cardio involved so we get very cold. We decided we wouldn't do this winter in the UK. We'd go away. We could also do promotions in America.

I think, ultimately, we will crack America. We're starting to get known by some people out there and I believe we can do it. I mean, what does 'cracked' even mean? There's always more fans you can get, even in England. But I think we can do well in the States.

We're always trying to push. If it's a possibility for us to crack America, we must do it. I don't want to have regrets when I'm 70 years old. Sitting on my rocking chair, bending the ears of my grandchildren about how I could have been big in America if I'd only tried.

We're giving it our best shot. This doesn't mean we've forgotten our English fans. We see ourselves as a global thing – we love our fans wherever you are.

The NBC show we filmed is *It's Called Football*. We filmed it in England for American viewers. We took free kicks with Dimitri Payet and Manuel Lanzini. We also met youth team players – up-and-coming players at West Ham and Chelsea. We examined the history of Southampton FC and learned about their current scouting methods.

It was fun. There's something about being on mainstream TV. YouTube has half taken over from TV in this generation. TV is probably on the way down. But it still feels like a symbol of success, having your own TV show. People can think: well, okay, you're good enough for YouTube but you're not good enough for TV.

Having your own TV series is big. It kind of makes you feel that you are proven, that you can back it up. So, YouTube is not your restriction or your limit. You can make it in the mainstream, too. Do you know what I mean by that?

I also think it's quite nice for the older ones in our fan base to have access to us on a more familiar platform

for them. Even middle-aged mums and elderly people have started to notice us. Suddenly, we have all sorts of people coming up to us on the street: mums, dads, grandparents. So, you can sense that being on normal TV opens us up to a wider audience.

We met American football star Odell Beckham Jr. He's such a cool guy. I raced him on the ladders. I think I could have gone faster than I did, but not faster than him. He's just so rapid, it's outrageous! He's a proper athlete, man. He can throw the ball so hard. We did some actual football kicking with him. He had an unusual technique but managed to get one – top bins.

I'd like to do more of this sort of video – videos with people who are famous in spheres outside football. We did Odell, so let's do Justin Bieber or Barack Obama or Drake. These type of collaborations – people would like to see them. I don't see why The F2 can't be the medium for people to see these videos. People will want to see Drake try a free kick or Obama taking a penalty.

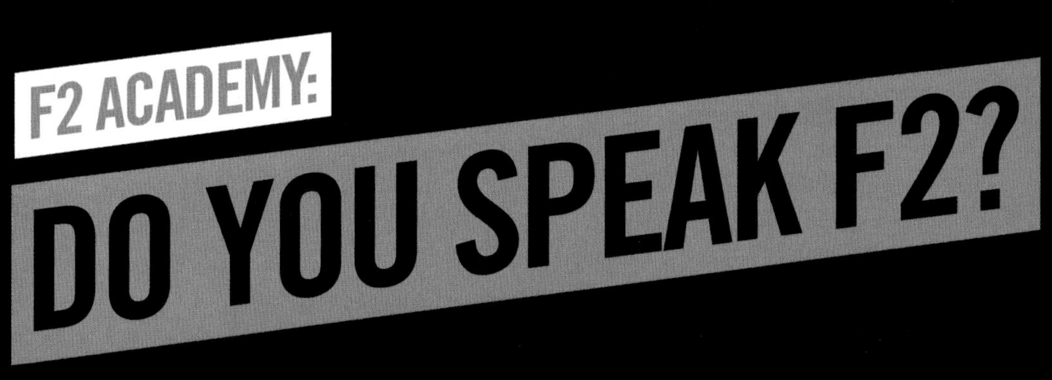

As you walk the walk, you'll also want to talk the talk. So, here's our guide to talking with tekkers. Drop some of these babies into your conversation and you'll be on top of the chat game.

SWAZ

Swaz is the bend you put on a ball that makes it move in the air. But it also can be used for anything that is cool. A great goal? Swaz. A fancy trick? Swaz. A blinding assist? Swaz. It's a great word. We use it a lot. Sweet as!

WHIPPAGE

A great way of emulating the main man – Lionel Messi.

ELECTRIC TWIST

Bill invented this trick. It starts with a step-over, continues with a feint, and finishes with a drag-back and twist. You can absolutely destroy defenders with this one because just as they think they know what you are doing, you go the other way.

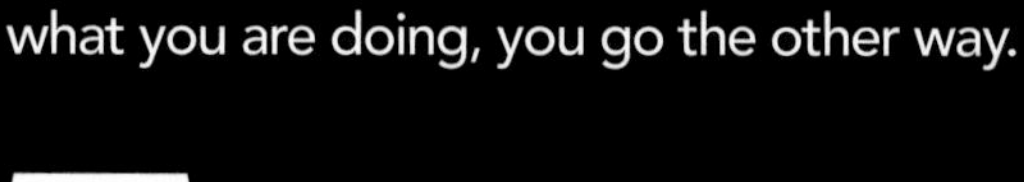

AKKA

Jez invented this skill. You roll the sole of your foot over the ball to flick it up, bounce it off the outside of your calf and then toe it past the defender, before speeding past him. If you want to learn more about The F2 Akka, see our first book, *F2 World of Football*.

LIBERO

Sometimes known as the 'sweeper', the libero is a special kind of centre-back who takes a fluid approach to the game. They will 'sweep up' and usually have flair and passing panache over and above what you'd expect from a defender.

NO-LOOK PASS

Ronaldinho was the king of this. This might look like mere showing off to some fans, but it can get you a major advantage in some situations. Anyway, what's wrong with a bit of showing off? There's a place for it!

BACK SNAP

Another skill that was invented by The F2. You flick the ball up, turn your back on the ball, lift your leg and bend your knee, before kicking the leg backwards and pinging the ball off the back of your knee.

BANTER

You've got to have a bit of fun when you're playing and practising with your mates. Keep it fair and keep it fun.

FLICK

Sometimes you want a hard pass, sometimes you want a soft pass. But when you want a really cheeky pass, you can't do better than a flick. Watch the most skilled players, they will have great flickage ability in the old locker!

F2 ACADEMY:

INSTEP

So many important skills see you strike the ball with your instep. Whippage is one of them. Never neglect this part of your football boot, people!

TOP BINS

The top corner of the goal. It's what you shout when you've smashed a shot that's given the keeper no chance at all.

JOG ON

If you don't like top-notch football then you've come to the wrong place, guys. So, jog on!

ONE-TOUCH

If you want to tiki-taka as a team then you've got to work on your one-touch passing. It's hard to get right, particularly in the pressure of a match situation, but when it comes off it's great to see and lethal too.

RABONA

Invented in the 1940s in Argentina, the Rabona sees you whip your striking leg round the back of your standing leg. It looks breath-taking.

TEKKERS

This is the most important word in The F2 vocabulary because it's what we're all about: great technique. Love, peace and tekkers to you all!

CHEST TRAP

Watch players like Alexis Sánchez pull this baby off. Wanna try it? Get up on your toes and stretch your arms out to get some balance. Then you just lean back and let the ball sink into your chest.

YES GUYS!

The words that have launched a hundred F2 videos. It's like our little greeting and it works for us. Yes guys!

TEKKERS MASTERS: PIERRE-EMERICK AUBAMEYANG

'LEGEND HAS IT HE'S THE QUICKEST PLAYER IN THE WORLD.'

Jez: We literally love this man.

Billy: We do. He's very friendly and also a funny guy – a really, really funny guy. He doesn't take himself seriously at all, which for a player of his calibre is admirable. Sometimes top stars in any walk of life get a bit overserious about themselves, but not him. When we filmed a commercial with him, he made a lot of jokes. A lot of really outrageous jokes. They were a bit rude, so we can't really put them in here, can we?

Jez: I dunno, can we?

Billy: No. Definitely, no. He made so many jokes all the time, even while we were being filmed. We struggled to keep a straight face.

Jez: Back to the football, though. Legend has it he's the quickest player in the world. I think that's actually probably true. I want to get him to race us two – just to compare. I mean, we know he will win, but we'll want to see what the gap is. There would be no shame in losing to him in a race. It would just be good to measure ourselves against him. To see how close we could get.

Billy: He's probably the player with the most flair at the moment. There aren't exactly tonnes of this sort of player about currently, but he is just phenomenal. He's lightning-quick, a top, top-class finisher.

Jez: I know he started out as a winger and you can see that in his play now. He's dynamic in all attacking positions,

'HE DOES HIS STEP-OVERS, HIS BURSTS OF DRIBBLING AND HE'S SO STRONG IN ONE-ON-ONE SITUATIONS.'

but most of all it's his pace that does the damage. He absolutely terrorises opponents with it. He dovetails well with creative midfielders. Stick him in a side with one and watch them fly!

I love watching him play: he does his step-overs, his bursts of dribbling and he's so strong in one-on-one situations. He's deadly, because if you stick too close to him he can just turn you. But then you can't afford to step off him, either!

One thing that he doesn't always get enough credit for is his defensive work. How many talented attackers really put a shift in defensively? Not many. Alexis Sánchez is one. Auba is another. He's like the first line of defence, running at the opposition back four and harrying their goalkeeper.

It shows you his commitment and his will to win. He wants to do it all because that's how badly he wants to win. This pressing isn't just showboating, trying to impress the fans. Watch how he does it: it's considered and poised. It's more than sweat – it's smart.

That combination of brains and brawn has seen him win trophies and also personal honours. He won the

African Footballer of the Year award in 2015 and was named in the top-ten players in the world overall. It doesn't surprise me, man. Not at all.

Billy: He likes filming with us and we DM with him on Twitter sometimes. I'm begging him to come to the Prem. He's a flair player who really excites you. If you're a football fan you are going to love to watch this guy play. Plus, anyone who wants to play the game can learn so much from him.

He's also a style icon off the pitch, where he likes to dress really boldly. He's a bit like Pogba in that way.

Jez: He wears Rascal clothing, he DMs us, as Bill said. He's always been really supportive of us. He's up for a laugh. Yeah, a really, really nice man.

Billy: When we did that 'workmen' video with him, Hummels and Schmelzer it was a real buzz. Just doing tricks in front of them was an honour. We love what we do and days like that are among the highlights. To be able to connect with some of the best talent on the planet, we feel lucky.

Jez: We do, we feel blessed.

GET THE SKILLS: TRIVELA

FACT FILE

ORIGIN: UNKNOWN
SKILL TYPE: SHOT
DIFFICULTY RATING: 6
TEKKERS RATING: 8
FREQUENTLY USED BY: RICARDO QUARESMA, ANDREA PIRLO, ROBERTO CARLOS

Jez: If this book is the academy, then we've just hit recess – it's time for some fun. This one is all about the swaz. I love a Trivela – the way the ball moves and swerves when you catch it just right. If you want to hit a pearler like Pirlo, or bend a free-kick like Roberto Carlos (look him up), then this is the move for you.

The key to hitting the perfect Trivela is to strike the ball with the outside of your boot. But, most importantly, you need to follow all the way through. That's what turns your swerve to swaz and your textbook to tekkers. Right, that's it, ding-ding, lunch break's over – time to get back to the practice pitch and put in the hard yards.

F2
RUN UP STRAIGHT
STRIKE THE BOTTOM OF THE BALL
WITH THE OUTSIDE OF YOUR BOOT
FOLLOW THROUGH HIGH FOR
MAXIMUM BEND

USE THE OUTSIDE OF YOUR BOOT

STRAIGHT RUN

HEAD DOWN TO HELP CONTROL DIRECTION

STRIKE THE BOTTOM SIDE OF THE BALL
BOOM

adidas
adidas

F2
CHAPTER
TEN

F2 ACADEMY:

COMING SOON F2: GALAXY OF FOOTBALL

Yes guys! Here's an exclusive look at a very exciting project that we're working on right now: our own graphic novel! It's coming out soon, but you guys get to see it ahead of everyone else.

There's football, good-guys, bad-guys, aliens trying to take over the world, time-travel, and some of the best footballers in the galaxy. Enjoy!

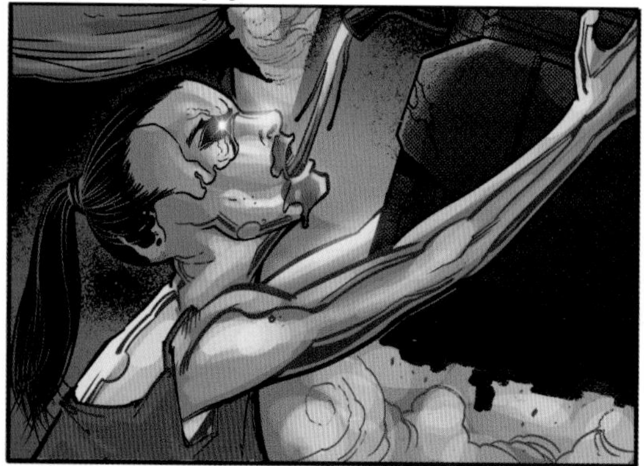

NOW I CAN PLAY WITH FOOTBALL ACROSS ALL OF TIME AND SPACE.
UMM... YOU MEAN NOW YOU CAN PLAY FOOTBALL ACROSS ALL OF TIME AND SPACE, RIGHT?
NO.
THAT'S NOT ON!
YOU DON'T GET TO TAKE OVER FOOTBALL.
OR, YOU KNOW ... THE HUMAN RACE, BILL.
WHAT? OH... YEAH, THAT TOO.
EITHER WAY, IT'S NOT ON!
YOU WISH... TO OPPOSE ME..?

HAHAHA!!
WONDERFUL. A NEW GAME... OF COURSE... WE SHALL PLAY.
RIGHT. A GAME THEN. A FOOTBALL GAME. OUR TEAM AGAINST YOURS.
BUT IF WE WIN, YOU GO HOME. YOU LET EARTH'S PEOPLE GO.
AND IF... I WIN?
THEN THERE'S NOT MUCH ELSE WE CAN DO TO STOP YOU THEN, IS THERE?
YOU'LL HAVE ALL OF TIME AND SPACE TO CONQUER.
THAT SOUNDS ... GOOD TO ME. OF COURSE...
YOU MAY FIND IT ... DIFFICULT... TO ASSEMBLE A TEAM ... WHO CAN OPPOSE ME.
NAH, MATE. EASY DONE.
THERE'S A LOT OF YOU, SURE. BUT YOU DON'T HAVE THE TEKKERS.
THE WHAT?

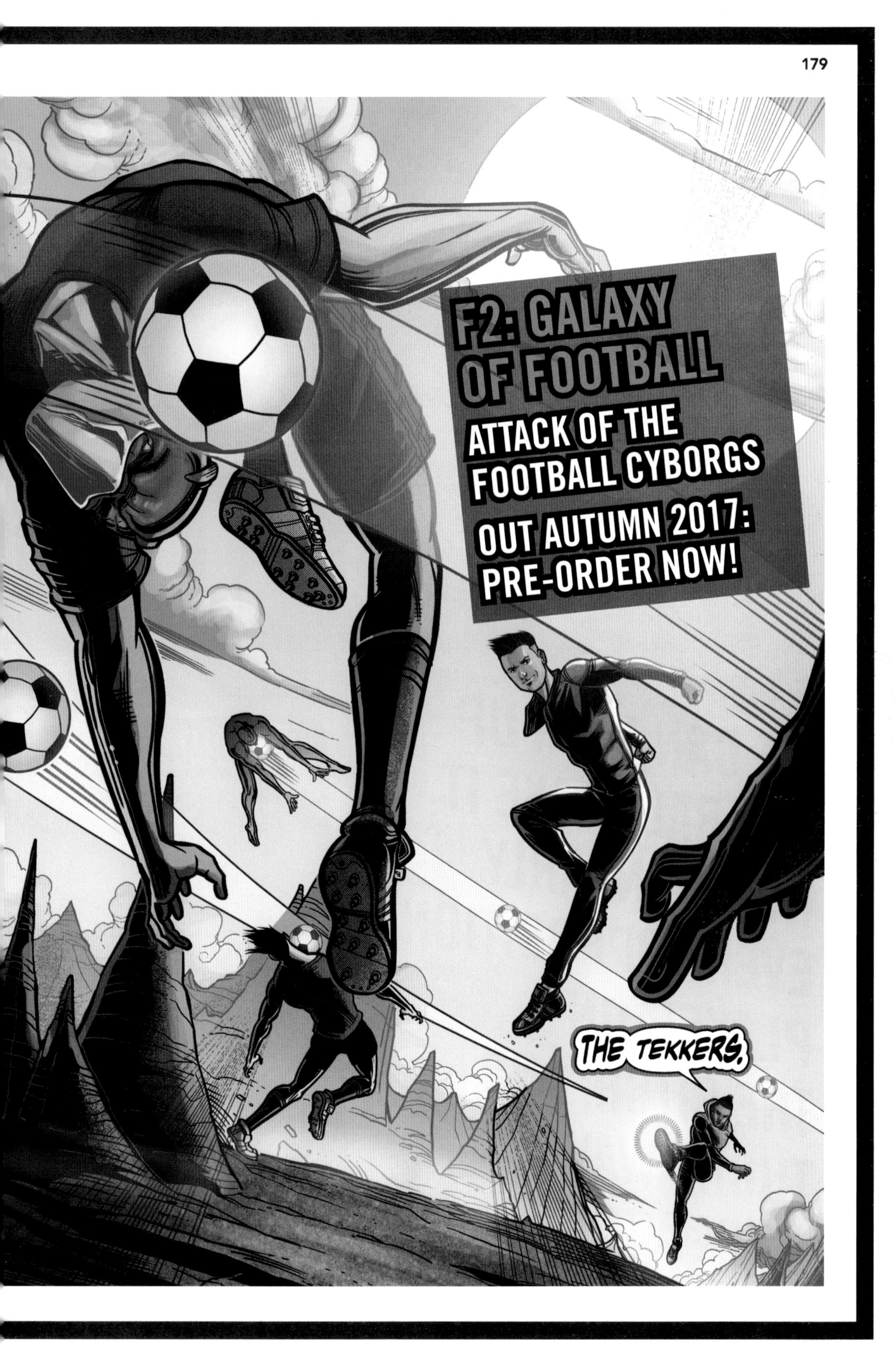
F2: GALAXY OF FOOTBALL
ATTACK OF THE FOOTBALL CYBORGS
OUT AUTUMN 2017: PRE-ORDER NOW!
THE TEKKERS.

TEKKERS MASTERS:

DIEGO MARADONA

'HE CAN PICK UP THE BALL, TAKE IT ROUND NEARLY EVERY OPPOSITION PLAYER ON THE PITCH, AND TUCK AWAY A SWEET GOAL.'

Jez: Ah, the Argentinian legend. I made a film in search of him, of course. It was a five-week quest to meet Diego Maradona. I was the only one who didn't get to meet him, ironically. I still to this day haven't met him, which is a bit gutting.

Look, as a player he's a pioneer. He's like a version of Lionel Messi in a different era. Though, actually, thinking about it I'd say Messi is slightly better than him. Controversial, I know.

Diego was a groundbreaker in the game. Before he came along, there wasn't another player who was like him. Messi is like Maradona, but Maradona was like no one else before him.

Billy: Yeah, what can we say about this guy that hasn't been said a million times before? He can pick up the ball, take it round nearly every opposition player on the pitch and tuck away a sweet goal. Even if he gets kicked up in the air, he just carries on. No rolling around. At his best, he's unstoppable. He's got that low centre of gravity that guys like Messi and Agüero have.

He's a man who single-handedly invented freestyling, almost by accident. You'd see him balancing the ball on his head and his neck. We take all that for granted now. Freestyling is just a thing. He started it, though. He's like an inventor – the entrepreneur of football skills.

Jez: Yeah, he was one of the first freestylers. In his head, he's invented something that didn't even exist.

How absolutely sick is that? He's like a magician. He was even unreal during the pre-match warm-up for matches. The crowd would be watching him doing his tricks and they'd be cheering. You can find videos of all that on YouTube. It must have been such an experience to be there in person, though.

Billy: He was a one-off in his era, a one-off in football history, really. I just wish that he played in this era. How fascinating would it be to see him in the Premier League or in the Champions League? How do you guys think he would fare?

'HIS DRIBBLING WAS MESMERIC.'

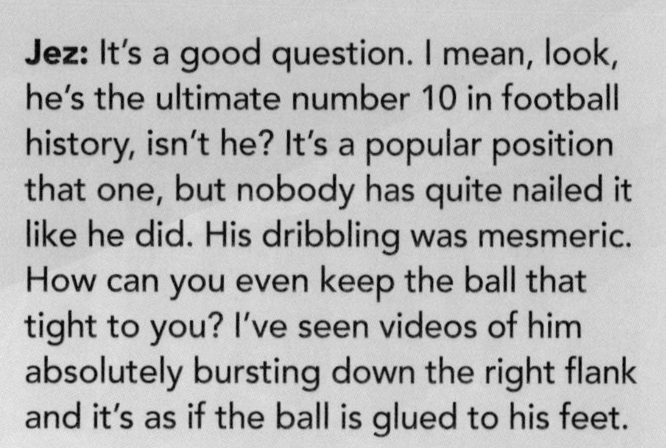

Jez: It's a good question. I mean, look, he's the ultimate number 10 in football history, isn't he? It's a popular position that one, but nobody has quite nailed it like he did. His dribbling was mesmeric. How can you even keep the ball that tight to you? I've seen videos of him absolutely bursting down the right flank and it's as if the ball is glued to his feet.

Billy: Yeah, and that's unstoppable for defenders. How do you stop a man with that control, and with that compact physique? You've just got to go out there, do your best and hope that he doesn't make you look too daft!

Jez: Ha, ha – fingers crossed on that one! I know he's sometimes been devastating to England, but that's not something to worry about now. Football is a universal love. Even though he scored that amazing goal when he dribbled from the halfway line against England, as well as that famous, controversial goal with his hand, we still love him because he's just got so much class. It's down to his footballing ability and what he brings to the game.

Billy: We've met Pelé but, as Jez said, he hasn't met Maradona and neither have I. He's definitely a man we would love to meet and film with. It would be amazing to see what he can do with the ball now. Really, in a way, we owe him a lot because as we've said, he kind of invented tekkers and freestyling.

Jez: So here's a shout out – Diego Maradona, we want to film with you! We've filmed with Pelé and now we want you. Any chance, legend?

GET THE SKILLS: WINGROVE HOUDINHO

FACT FILE

ORIGIN: NEW EXCLUSIVE SKILL!
INVENTED BY BILLY WINGROVE, UK
SKILL TYPE: DRIBBLE
DIFFICULTY RATING: 10
TEKKERS RATING: 10
FREQUENTLY USED BY: MR B. WINGROVE

Billy: So, it's the final day of The F2 Academy. You have exams, but you've studied hard and you want that 'A'. Hey, you've earned that 'A'. You open your paper and you're confronted with this: The Wingrove Houdinho. Pop quiz, hotshot: what would you do?!

This move is so next-level, you're gonna have to forget taking the stairs, or the lift and or even a helicopter. This move is mile-high, in the sky, eating apple pie on your way to Dubai. You're going to need to break this down into two moves. First, practise the flick. Once you've nailed that, work on the back heel. Then try it in a game. Practise, practise, practise – it's time for your graduation day. I know you're going to make it.

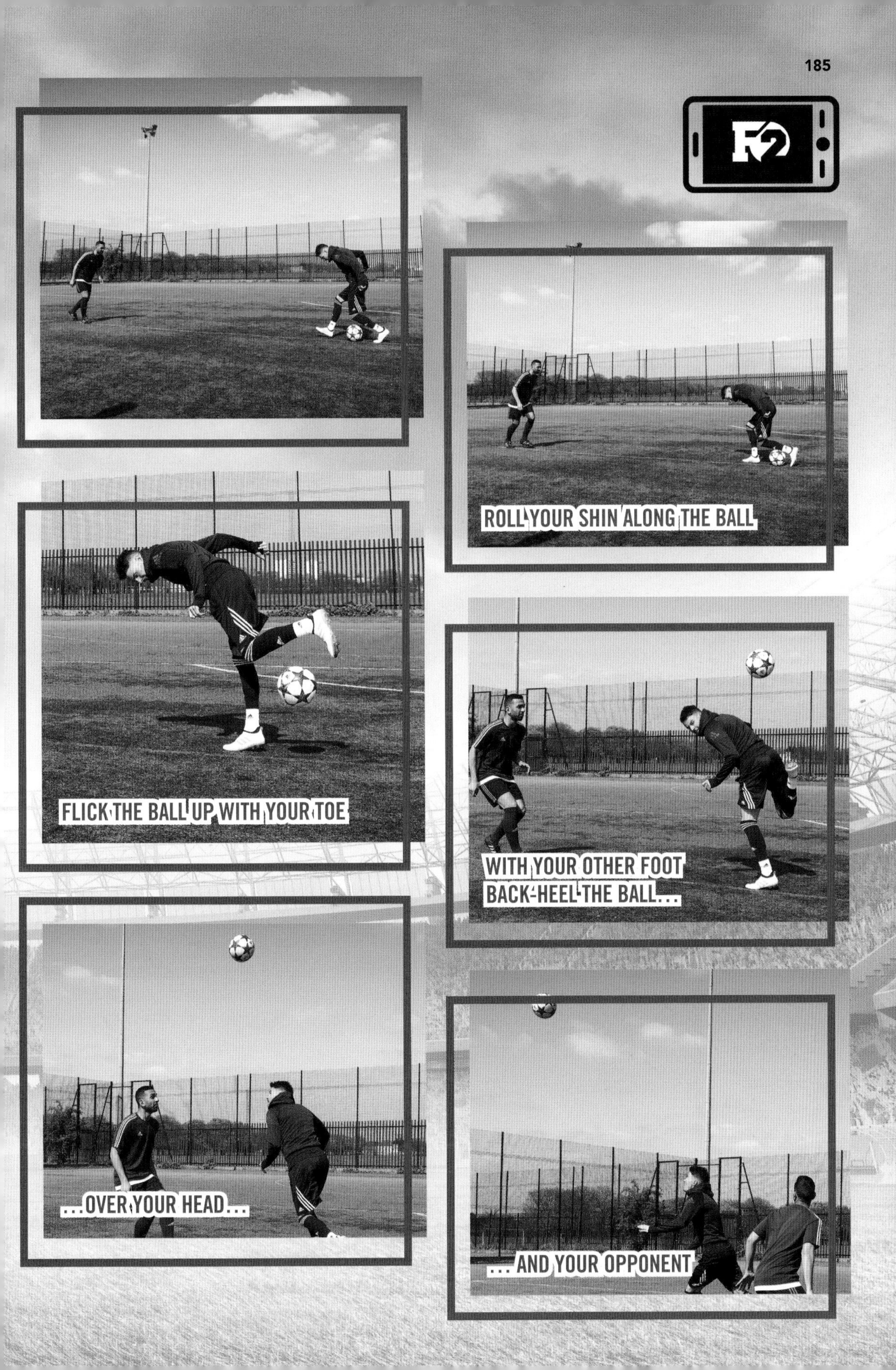
F2
ROLL YOUR SHIN ALONG THE BALL
FLICK THE BALL UP WITH YOUR TOE
WITH YOUR OTHER FOOT
BACK-HEEL THE BALL...
...OVER YOUR HEAD...
...AND YOUR OPPONENT

ROLL THE BALL BACK BY PULLING YOUR KNEE BACK

PUT PRESSURE ON TOP OF THE BALL WITH YOUR SHIN...

FLICK WITH YOUR TOE

LIFT YOUR LEG UP AND FOLLOW THE BALL

WITH THE BALL IN THE AIR, BACK-HEEL IT OVER YOUR HEAD WITH YOUR OTHER FOOT

F2 OUTRO

So here comes the final whistle.

What have we learned during this book? If there is one lesson we would love you to take away, it is that setbacks happen. Whether it's an injury, an epic fail or a huge tragedy – not everything is always going to go your way.

We even saw how players like Paul Pogba and Gerard Piqué were rejected. How little guys like Alexis Sánchez and Sergio Agüero had to prove themselves while surrounded by guys who were giants in comparison.

Yet they all came through. That's why determination and belief are vital. Never stop believing in yourselves, guys, and always give everything your very best shot. What more can we ask of you than that?

Enjoy football – it's brilliant!

Love, peace, and tekkers, The F2

RASCAL
FINAL
RASCALCLOTHING.COM
#BeRascal
RASCAL

ACKNOWLEDGEMENTS

First of all, the people we'd like to thank most are our families, for looking out for us, supporting us and always being there for us. There have been some amazing and exciting opportunities in the last year, but there have also been some tough times to deal with. We've been through it all together and come through the other side. Thanks and much love to you all.

We'd like to say a big thank you to the team at Blink Publishing, including our editors Matt Phillips and Joel Simons; designers Steve Leard and Nathan Balsom; Joanna de Vries and Justine Taylor; not to forget Perminder Mann, Ben Dunn, Andrew Sauerwine, Lisa Hoare, Lizzie Dorney-Kingdom, Beth Eynon, Alba Proko, Ahmad Farooq and Zoe Fawcett. The book couldn't have been made without Chas Newkey-Burden, and the pictures from Dan Rouse and Chris Macchi, thanks so much guys.

Big thanks too, to all the brands and teams within the agencies who have chosen to work with us. They are all such a core part of what we do; we couldn't do it without you. A particular shout-out to the team at Adidas, who have been there since the beginning.

A massive thank you also to all the teams, players and fellow YouTubers who have been part of our incredible videos and a key part of our unforgettable journey.

Lastly, a big shout out to all you guys – The F2 Family. Where would we be without your support? Thanks for all the memories. See you on the pitch.

PHOTOGRAPHY CREDITS

All images courtesy of The F2, except the following:

Dan Rouse:
6–7, 20–21, 28–31, 57, 64–67, 68–69, 82–85, 90, 100–101, 139, 140, 141, 150–153, 163, 184–187

Chris Macchi:
10–11, 12–13, 32–33, 38–39, 44–47, 48–49, 51, 52–53, 54, 55, 86–87, 89, 91, 92–93, 102–103, 116–119, 120-121, 132–135, 136–137, 154–155, 157, 158, 159, 160, 161, 164, 165, 170–173, 174–175, 188–189

Getty Images:
15, 18, 21, 22, 23, 24, 25, 26, 27, 36, 37 40, 41, 42, 43, 56, 57, 58, 59, 60, 61, 62, 63, 74, 75, 76, 77, 78, 79, 80, 81, 94, 95, 96, 97, 98, 99, 105, 106, 107, 108, 109, 110, 111, 112, 113, 115, 126, 127, 128, 129, 130, 131, 142, 143, 145, 146, 147, 148, 149, 162, 163, 165, 166, 167, 168, 169, 180, 181, 182, 183